Ride Your Bike

GW00514821

Contents

How to use this guide

The *Ride Your Bike* guides are designed for riders of all levels: from complete novices and those with a little experience to people that have been cycling all their lives.

Chapter 1 aims to whet the appetite for the area covered by the guide. As well as general information about the geological character and history of the region, places of interest are identified and described.

Chapter 2 provides important basic information on preparing yourself and your bike before a ride, getting to the start of a route, navigation skills, as well as advice on safety and emergencies.

If you would like to know more about bikes, equipment, repair and maintenance and travelling further afield into Europe and the rest of the world, *Mountain Biking*, *The Bike Book* and *Fix Your Bike* are published by Haynes and available from all good bike and bookshops.

A locator map is included on pages 4-5 for easy identification of rides in your area. The ride facts chart at the back of the guide is designed to provide key information 'at a glance' to make selecting a ride that suits your mood, energy level and degree of expertise simple and quick.

© Crown Copyright

The guide contains 19 rides graded easy, medium and difficult.

Easy rides are for novices, families with young children and for people who are getting back into riding after a gap. They are relatively short and use good surfaces such as dismantled railways. You don't need any expertise to do these rides, just the enthusiasm to get out there.

Medium rides are a little more challenging in terms of distance and terrain. If you have done all the easy routes, have built up some confidence and mastered the basic trail techniques try one of the shorter routes in this category. You will soon feel able to try the rest. Check through the directions to alert yourself to anything you may not be able to manage.

Difficult rides are for the experienced mountain biker and demand a good command of trail techniques, fitness and more than a dash of courage. They are exciting and challenging and great fun. Make sure you and your bike are in good shape before you contemplate a difficult route: they often go into remote areas and use challenging terrain.

Locator map

The map below gives the approximate location of each ride featured in the guide. The rides are numbered 1 through to 19, 1 being an easy route and 19 a hard route with all the others in sequence in between. Once you have located a ride in the area in which you are interested turn to the back and check its suitability on the Ride Facts at a Glance chart.

1 Appledore
2 The Meon Valley
3 Along the Cuckoo Trail
4 The Basingstoke Canal

5 Downs Link one
6 Downs Link two
7 Bedgebury
8 Around Bewl Water

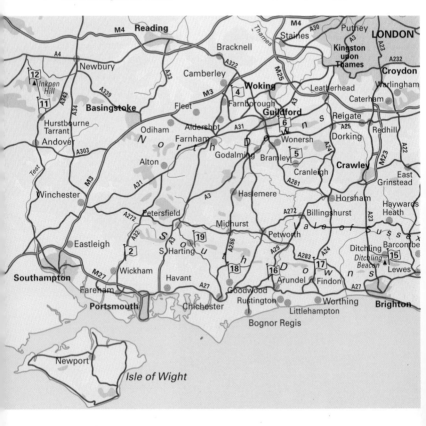

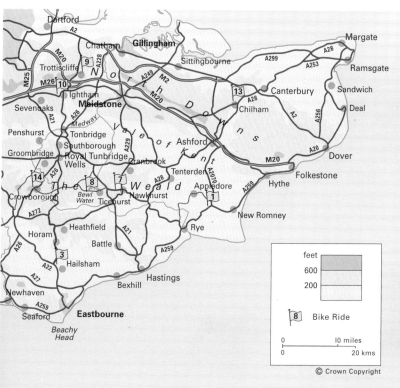

Chapter 1: Introduction to the area

F ROM KENT, 'the garden of England', with its oast houses, orchards of fruit trees and glorious springtime blossom, to the dramatic whaleback ridge of the South Downs giving far-reaching views out to the English Channel; from the sandy heathland and pine forests of Surrey to the rich, rolling farmland of Hampshire, there is an intimate feel to the countryside of southeast England which conceals constant surprises.

Fragments of the ancient broadleaf forest of Anderida still stand in the Wealden clay, neolithic burial mounds can be found along both the main chalk ridges of the region and the Romans, too, have left their mark in the form of palaces and roads. Since the last invasion from the continent, in 1066, the area has enjoyed remarkable stability and this is reflected in the varied architecture of church, castle, stately home, village and cottage spanning several centuries.

The oasthouses of Summerford Farm near Balls Green

For an area so densely populated and so close to one of the world's major cities, the counties south of London boast a surprisingly varied network of bridleways and quiet lanes, canals, dismantled railways and Forestry Commission holdings. Combined, these features offer a wide choice of cycling possibilities from easy family routes through to tough offroad challenges on the steep slopes of the South Downs. Add to this the achievements of two of the country's most progressive local authorities in the field of recreational cycling (Sussex and Hampshire) and you have a fine recipe for the exploration of this well-to-do corner of England.

Bluebell woods north of Wickham

The North Downs

THE CHALK RIDGE of the North Downs runs in a wide arc, west from the cliffs of Dover to the broader chalk beds of the Hampshire Downs west of Farnham, passing close to London parallel with the M25. For an area which is so built up it is surprising how quickly you can escape into the countryside.

The North Downs Way, from Farnham to Dover, follows an ancient track for 225 kms (140 miles), keeping as close to the summit of the North Downs as possible and rising to 294m/965ft at Leith Hill. In parts it coincides with the Pilgrims Way, so-called because it is thought to have been used by pilgrims travelling to the shrine of Thomas à Becket at Canterbury. Its status varies between footpath and bridleway so that you cannot ride along its entire length. However, there are several bases along the North Downs around which there is a good network of legal trails. From west to east they are: Gomshall, Peaslake, Leith Hill, Walton on the Hill, Limpsfield and Wye.

An avenue of trees on the Fairlawne Estate, near Plaxtol

Places to visit

Winkworth Arboretum is 100 acres of hillside covered with azaleas and bluebells, rare trees and shrubs, best seen in spring and autumn. **Box Hill**, named after the trees that grew here, has been a popular viewpoint and picnic spot since the reign of Charles II. **Leith Hill Tower**, the highest point in southeast England, was built by the local landowner Richard Hull in 1766. **Chartwell** was **Sir Winston Churchill**'s family home for more than 40 years. **Ightham Mote** (*see* ride no 10) is a perfect medieval moated manor house set in a secluded valley. The hall was built in the 14th century and the stonework in the courtyard forms a Tudor rose. The history of **Leeds Castle** goes back 1000 years. The lake-bound castle is set in the sublime grounds landscaped by **Capability Brown** who also designed the gardens of **Chilham Castle,** a Jacobean mansion whose grounds also contain a ruined Norman keep. **The White Cliffs Experience**, Dover, recreates the whole pageant of Dover's history from Roman times to the evacuation of Dunkirk and the Battle of Britain.

The Great Stour valley and the North Downs south of Chilham

Rides in this area featured in the book: Downs Link one and two, Trottiscliffe and Coldrum Long Barrow, Ightham Mote, King's Wood

A chalk and flint bridleway near Charlton, typical of the South Downs

The South Downs

THE SOUTH DOWNS are compact and contained almost within one county, Sussex. The chalk ridge seldom rises above 240m/800ft, but it is nevertheless majestic, culminating at Beachy Head, rising 160m/534ft sheer from the waters of the English Channel. The well-defined 80-mile long South Downs Way stretches from Eastbourne to Buriton, following the ridge of the Downs within sight of the sea for almost all its length. Its bridleway status makes it one of the longest waymarked offroad cycling trails in England. There are five highpoints along the South Downs ridge where the views are especially far-reaching: Firle Beacon, Ditchling Beacon, Chanctonbury Ring, Bignor Hill and Beacon Hill. On a fine day with good visibility these hilltops are some of the most magical places in the whole of Southern England.

Places to visit

Chichester is still laid out to the original Roman plan. Surrounded by city walls it contains a Norman cathedral, a 15th-century market cross and fine Georgian architecture. **Bignor** village is the site of a 65-room Roman villa with superb mosaics and the Roman road of **Stane Street** (see ride no 16), runs nearby. **Arundel** is famous for its castle, the ancestral home of the Dukes of Norfolk, completed after the Norman Conquest to defend the Arun valley. The town also contains a Toy and Military Museum and **Arundel Wildfowl and Wetlands Trust** is nearby. **Cissbury Ring** is an impressive Iron Age hill fort built about 300 BC. The site was used by Stone Age man to mine flints and remains of burial mounds can be seen. Legend has it that **Devil's Dyke** near Steyning, a deep hollow on the Downs above Brighton, was dug by the Devil to flood the Weald with the English Channel and frustrate the growth of Christianity. **Lewes**, the county town of East Sussex, is full of fine buildings of all periods; medieval streets and a Norman Castle. No one knows the identity of the 72m/240ft **Long Man of Wilmington**, cut into the Downs near the village of Wilmington. He was possibly the work of Iron Age man.

Rides in this area featured in the book: Arundel to Bignor Hill, Ditchling Beacon to Lewes, Glorious Goodwood, Chanctonbury Ring from Findon, Harting Downs

A leafy path southeast of Stoughton

The Hampshire Downs

T HE HAMPSHIRE DOWNS are part of the great chalk beds radiating from Salisbury. Mainly gentle and rolling in character, their highpoint is at Walbury Hill (297m/974ft) and Inkpen Beacon (291m/954ft) the highest chalk hills in England. The area around Alton is where the North and South Downs meet. Old drove roads and tracks cross-cross the hills, some of which have been incorporated into the area's two principal long distance trails, the Wayfarers Walk and the the Test Way.

As well as the rides in this guide, of interest to the cyclist are the Forestry Commission holdings at North Boarhunt to the north of Fareham, in Queen Elizabeth Park to the southwest of Petersfield and those located to the north and west of Farnborough and Camberley.

Barges on the Basingstoke Canal near Brookwood

Places to visit

Winchester, the royal capital of Saxon Wessex and of England until the late 12th century, was regarded by the Tudors as the site of Arthur's Camelot. A fine medieval Great Hall is the sole remnant of the castle, begun in 1067 and rebuilt by Henry III, and is complete with a round table. **Winchester Cathedral** was begun in 1079 for William the Conqueror and contains the bones of pre-Norman kings including Canute. Train enthusiasts will want to visit the **mid-Hants Railway**, which boasts two stations restored to their former steam-age glory and a steam train running along the 'Watercress Line', so named because it was used by growers to get produce to market. **Watership Down**, the beauty spot that inspired Richard Adams' novel, lies to the west of Kingsclere and in **Whitchurch** you can still see garments being woven using traditional techniques. **Jane Austen** lived in Chawton and the village contains an exhibition of her life and works. Selborne was home to the pioneer naturalist **Gilbert White** (1720-93). His house is now a museum devoted to his work.

Lush spring greenery on the Meon Valley Way, south of Soberton

Rides in this area featured in the book: Inkpen Hill, Hurstbourne Tarrant, The Basingstoke Canal, The Meon Valley

The Weald

To PICTURE THE GEOLOGY of the country south of London imagine a claw holding a ball: the North Downs are the forefinger, the South Downs are the thumb and the High Weald is the ball in the middle, made of hard rocks which were once covered with a vast cap of chalk. As the chalk eroded it revealed the underlying greensand beds.

Formerly covered by the huge primeval Forest of Anderida, the High Weald rises to 236m/788ft near Crowborough. Either side of the High Weald lie beds of clay little loved by offroad cyclists - unbelievably sticky in the winter and baked into hard corrugations in the summer. Luckily the railway paths, reservoirs, some Forestry Commission holdings and a good network of quiet lanes provide enjoyable alternatives.

Places to visit

High Beech, south of Crawley, has woodland and water gardens and a wildflower meadow which is a magnet to butterflies. **The Bluebell Railway** between Horsted Keynes and Sheffield Park has a collection of locomotives and rolling stock dating from between 1865 and 1958. There is also the **Kent & East Sussex Railway** which runs southwest from Tenterden. **A.A. Milne** lived in Hartfield, a village with two ancient inns, a 13th-century church and houses built between the 16th and 18th centuries. **Christopher Robin** and **Pooh** played Poohsticks in neighbouring **Ashdown Forest**. The Great Hall of **Penshurst Place**, one of the great houses of England, was built in 1340. There are impressive apartments, an armour collection, a toy museum and an adventure playground. Nearby is the authentic Tudor village of **Chiddingstone** which has been featured in many period films. **Bodiam Castle**, a picture-book castle built in the 14th century, is still

Rides in this area featured in the book: Forest Way, Around Bewl Water, Bedgebury, The Cuckoo Trail, Appledore and Romney Marsh

remarkably intact and boasts rounded corner towers, battlements, portcullis and a moat. Restored traction engines are on display at the **Quarry Farm Steam Museum**. **Rye** is an ancient port and was home to the American novelist **Henry James**. A town of cobbled streets and timbered houses, it is the site of the 12th-century **Ypres Tower**, built to defend the town, and also the **Mermaid Inn**, in the past a haunt of smugglers.

A typical Kent oasthouse on the Trottiscliffe route

Local amenities

For up-to-date information about accommodation (including a booking service), places to visit, public transport timetables and local events Tourist Information Centres (listed below) offer an excellent service. An asterisk indicates that the centre is not open all year round. See pages 18-19 for their location.

Also listed below are cycle hire companies although the local information centres will have the most up to date information on where to hire bicycles.

Alton
7 Cross and Pillory Lane,
Alton, Hampshire GU34 1HL
Tel: 01420 88448

Andover
Town Mill House, Bridge Street,
Andover, Hampshire SP10 1BL
Tel: 01264 324320

Arundel
61 High Street, Arundel,
West Sussex BN18 9AJ
Tel: 01903 882268

Ashford
18 The Churchyard,
Ashford, Kent TN23 1QG
Tel: 01233 629165

Basingstoke
Willis Museum, Old Town Hall,
Market Place, Basingstoke,
Hampshire RG21 1QD
Tel: 01256 817618

Brighton
10 Bartholomew Square,
Brighton, East Sussex BN1 1JS
Tel: 01273 323755

Canterbury
34 St Margaret's Street,
Canterbury, Kent CT1 2TG
Tel: 01227 766567

Chichester
29a South Street, Chichester,
West Sussex. PO19 1AH
Tel: 01243 775888

Cranbrook *not open all year round*
Vestry Hall, Stone Street,
Cranbrook, Kent TN17 3HA
Tel: 01580 712538

Farnham
Vernon House, 28 West Street,
Farnham, Surrey GU9 7DR
Tel: 01252 715109

Fleet
The Harlington Centre,
Gurkha Square, Fleet Road,
Fleet, Hampshire GU13 8BY
Tel: 01252 811151

Guildford
14 Tunsgate, Guildford,
Surrey GU1 3QT
Tel: 01483 444007

Hailsham

The Library, Western Road,
Hailsham, East Sussex BN27 3DN
Tel: 01323 844426

Horsham

9 Causeway, Horsham,
West Sussex RH12 1HE
Tel: 01403 211661

Lewes

187 High Street, Lewes,
East Sussex BN7 2DE
Tel: 01273 483448

Maidstone

The Gatehouse, The Palace Gardens, Mill
Street, Maidstone, Kent ME15 6YE
Tel: 01622 673581

Newbury

The Wharf, Newbury,
Berkshire RG14 5AS
Tel: 01635 30267

Petersfield

County Library, 27 The Square,
Petersfield, Hampshire GU32 3HH
Tel: 01730 268829

Rye

The Heritage Centre, Strand Quay,
Rye, East Sussex TN31 7AY
Tel: 01797 226696

Sevenoaks

Buckhurst Lane, Sevenoaks,
Kent TN13 1LQ
Tel: 01732 450305

Tenterden

Town Hall, High Street, Tenterden,
Kent TN30 6AN
Tel: 01580 763572

Winchester

Guildhall, The Broadway,
Winchester, Hampshire SO23 9LJ
Tel: 01962 840500

Worthing

Chapel Road, Worthing,
West Sussex BN11 1HL
Tel: 01903 210022

Cycle Hire

Arundel

Arundel Cycle Hire
4 School Lane, Arundel, West Sussex
Tel: 01903 883712

Barcombe Mills

Take A Ride Cycle Hire
Station House, Barcombe Mills,
nr. Lewes, East Sussex BN8 5BL
Tel: 01273 400950

Bewl Water

(see under Cuckmere Cycle Company)

Brighton

On Your Bike (In Youth Hostel Shop)
126-127 Queens Road, Brighton East Sussex.
Tel: 01273 821369

Sunrise Cycle Hire, West Pier Promenade,
Kings Road, Brighton, East Sussex.
Tel: 01273 748881

Camberley

Wellington Trek
24 Wellington Road, Sandhurst,
Camberley, Surrey GU17 8AN.
Tel: 01344 772797

Canterbury

Canterbury Cycle Mart
19-23 Lower Bridge Street, Canterbury,
Kent CT1 2LG
Tel: 01227 761488

Chichester

Arun Bicycle Company
30b Southgate, South Street, Chichester
West Sussex PO19 1DP
Tel: 01243 537337

Cuckmere

Cuckmere Cycle Company
Forest Cycle Centre, The Barn, Seven
Sisters Country Park, Exceat, nr. Seaford,
East Sussex.
Tel: 01323 870310

They also take bookings for Bewl Water
and run the Cuckoo Cycle Centre in
Horam, tel 01435813000.

There is cycling for the disabled in the
forest from the Trekkers Disabled Cycling
Centre.

Farnham Alice Holt Forest

Woodland Park
(on A325 nr Bird World and the Forest
Gardening Centre) near Farnham
Tel: 01420 476612

Hailsham

Castle Cycle Hire
Queens University (Canada),
Herstmonceux Castle, Hailsham,
East Sussex BN27 0RP
Tel: 01323 833 537

Hastings

Hastings Cycle Hire and Sales
Above Saint Andrews Square Market,
South Terrace, Hastings, East Sussex
TN34 1SJ
Tel: 01424 444013

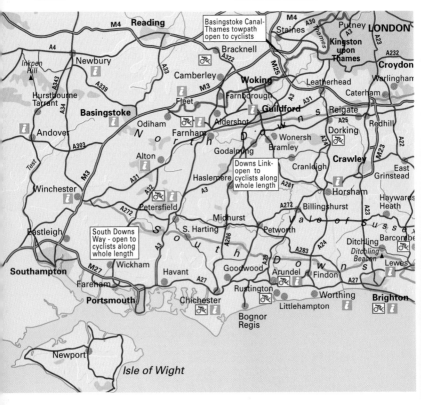

Penshurst

The Fir Tree Cycle Hire
Penshurst, Tonbridge, Kent TN11 8BB
Tel: 01892 870382

Petersfield

Queen Elizabeth Country Park nr
Petersfield, Hampshire
Tel: 0585 322849 (park) or 01705 591018

Rustington

Arun Bicycle Company
50 The Street, Rustington,
West Sussex BN16 3NR
Tel 01903 850418

Rye

Cyclonic, Shop 1
Corn Exchange, Strand Quay,
East Sussex TN31 7DB
Tel: 01797 223121

Rye Hire

Cyprus Place, Rye,
East Sussex TN31 7DR
Tel: 01797 223033

Surf Shack

Market Road, Rye, East
Sussex TN31 7JA
Tel: 01797 225746

West Humble

Action Packs
The Booking Hall, Box Hill Station,
West Humble Street, West Humble,
Surrey RH5 6BT
Tel: 01306 886944

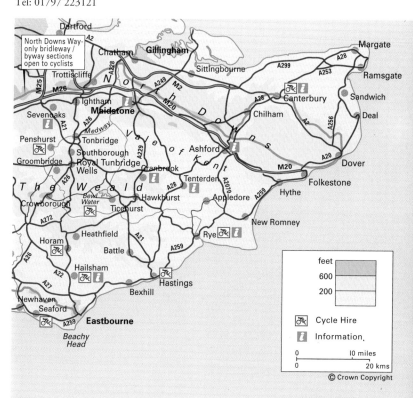

Weather and seasons

Trails

Off-road trails in the Downs and the Weald can be all but impossible from late autumn to late spring as the soil turns to sticky mud that cakes the tyres of your bike, picking up leaves and twigs and making riding anything but pleasurable. It is useful to note the location of garages with jet hoses that are either near to home or near to your favourite trails so that you can hose off the worst of the mud immediately after the ride.

In winter broad, stone-based tracks that are neither sunken nor enclosed by a canopy of vegetation tend to be the best to choose. This includes ridge sections of the South Downs Way. The other alternatives are Forestry Commission holdings, dismantled railways, quiet lanes and the geological strata of sandy, quick-draining Greensand Beds running parallel to and just south of the line of the North Downs.

Certain trails will be busier in the summer months but never so busy that they should be avoided. The best time for almost all of the rides in this guide is during May and June when the wildflowers are at their best and in mid-to late autumn when the colours of the leaves are changing. However, any fine day from the moment the trails have dried out (usually late April) to the onset of heavy winter rains (late-October/early November) is a good

Bedgebury Pinetum in early early summer, a perfect time for taking a trip

time to get out. Light summer evenings can be the very best time for short rides.

Winter

Days are much shorter in the winter, so even in southern England plan to have your ride finished by early to mid-afternoon. Don't be too ambitious, particularly on long rides on the South Downs: many accidents happen when people are determined to stick to a pre-set plan and who fail to alter their intended route to take account of the prevailing weather conditions. Having everything ready and getting an early start is essential in the winter.

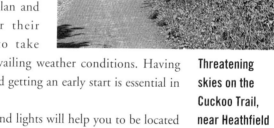

Threatening skies on the Cuckoo Trail, near Heathfield

Bright clothing and lights will help you to be located in the event of an accident and are vital on roads on those dark winter days when it never really seems to get light.

Forecasts

Weather forecasts vary considerably in accuracy, often the local forecast is very different to the national prediction, but the local forecasters should know best for their own area. Meteorologists now admit that one in five forecasts are wrong, so you have an 80 per cent chance of it being correct. Get as good a forecast as you can as close to your time of departure as possible. Telephone or fax forecasts are usually updated around 6am and provide the most up-to-date service available to the general public.

21

Family cycling

Traffic-free cycling on good surfaces is the key to enjoyable family cycling. The easy rides in chapter 3 are suitable for families. In addition the following areas are of interest. Details of facilities and the appropriate Ordnance Survey Landranger map are included.

Forestry Commission Holdings
Waymarked trails

Queen Elizabeth Park nr Petersfield (OS 197) The most developed of all the forestry areas in the region with bike hire, two waymarked trails, a visitor centre and easy links to the bridleway network in every direction.

West Walk, North Boarhunt, West Sussex (OS 196) Carpark, toilets, picnic site.

Friston Forest/Seven Sisters Country Park nr Eastbourne (OS 199) Cycle hire.

Alice Holt Forest nr Farnham (OS 186) Cycle hire.

Houghton Forest nr Arundel (OS 197) 3-mile trail, carpark, toilets, picnic site

For details of your nearest Forestry Commission holdings which operate an open access policy for cycling on the forestry tracks, write to the following addresses with a SAE:
Hampshire, Surrey, West Sussex - Forest Enterprise, West Downs District, Bucks Horn Oak, Farnham, Surrey GU10 4LS.
East Sussex and Kent - Forest Enterprise, Weald District, Goudhurst, Cranbrook, Kent TN17 2SL.

Dismantled railways and country parks

Downs Link (OS 187 and 198) The waymarked Downs Link continues south from Slinfold via Southwater, Partridge Green and Henfield to Steyning to link with the South Downs Way. There is a short road section between Slinfold and Southwater. (see ride nos 5 and 6)

The Worth Way (OS 187) A 5-mile trail starting just west of East Grinstead Station to Worth. There is a short road section through Crawley Down.

Forest Way (OS 187 and 188) It starts in and continues west from Forest Row to East Grinstead. (See ride 14).

Seven Sisters Country Park (OS 199) From Exceat, west of Eastbourne, flat cycling out to the coast alongside the River Cuckmere, plus Friston Forest.

Canals

Basingstoke Canal (OS 186 and 176) The canal runs from West Byfleet to Odiham. (See ride no 4). The Wey Navigation is not suitable for cycling except at the link section between the Basingstoke Canal and the Thames Towpath.

Kennet and Avon Canal, west of Reading (OS 174 and 175) Not the best surface. A 5.6 km (3½ mile) section either side of Aldermaston Wharf is rideable.

Royal Military Canal (OS 189) A 4.8 kms (3 mile) section west of Hythe has bridleway status.

Near London

Wimbledon Common, Putney Heath and Richmond Park (use the full colour A-Z guides) all have designated cycle trails.

The South Downs Way

Most of the South Downs Way is suitable only for reasonably fit mountain bikers. There are several flattish, linear sections along the ridge with magnificent views that are also rideable in summer on hybrid bikes or robust children's bikes.

Rackham Hill and Sullington Hill, south of Storrington (OS 197 and 198) between grid refs 051125 and 095117.

Chanctonbury Ring, west of Steyning (OS 198) between grid refs 163095 and 134120.

Devils Dyke, east of Steyning (OS 198) between grid refs 260106 and 220105.

Ditchling Beacon, south of Ditchling (OS 198) between grid refs 303134 and 374125.

Firle Beacon, southeast of Lewes (OS 198 and 199) between grid refs 455060 and 497048.

Designing a road route

Designing your own road route enables you to cycle all year round. It is also a good way of exploring an area without the mud and grime that affect off-road routes. You can ride with people with all types of bikes, carry children in bike seats and arrive at your destination looking reasonably presentable.

Planning a route from home

Start by deciding how far you want to go. Plan with the weakest person in mind. When pedalling along roads an average speed is 6-8 mph, therefore a 14-mile ride would be approximately two hours non-stop cycling. Each square on the Landranger 1:50,000 maps represents 1 kilometre or just over ½ mile so you can get a rough distance by counting the squares. Alternatively buy yourself a map measurer and run this over your intended route.

Decide whether you want to stop at a pub or teashop and what else you hope to visit

Decide on your destination then use a pen to mark out the best route

on the ride - a friend's house, a place of historic interest, a beauty spot for a picnic.

Check on the wind direction and listen to the weather forecast. You should try to cycle into the wind on the outward half of the ride and have it behind you on the return leg when you are more tired.

Planning in detail

Leisure cycling is as much about the travelling as the getting there so a lazy, meandering route on quiet lanes is likely to be more enjoyable than one which follows the quickest route between two points. Aim to:

- maximise time spent on quiet lanes and minimise time spent on main roads or busy lanes;
- avoid unnecessary steep hills;
- strike a balance between enjoying good views from high up, while not committing yourself to climbs beyond your capabilities;
- and decide whether the combination of refreshment stops, hills and wind means that the route is better undertaken clockwise or anti-clockwise.

With all this in mind and the appropriate Ordnance Survey Landranger map(s) spread out in front of you, mark the start point, your destination, places where you can cross the main roads (coloured red or brown) and link the dots using quiet lanes (marked yellow). Try to avoid roads with black arrows which indicate steep hills.

You may need to repeat part of the route, particularly the escape routes from large towns and cities such as canal towpaths, railway paths or designated cycle lanes, in order to minimise time on busy roads.

Network Southeast has adopted a more liberal approach than the rest of the country on transporting bikes so it is often possible to plan a route from a town/village in the counties around London. Choose a destination which can easily be linked to a network of yellow roads.

Below are some suggested starting points for road rides near to networks of lanes in Hampshire, Surrey, Sussex and Kent.

In Hampshire:
Bramley*
New Alresford
Odiham
Petersfield*
West Meon
Whitchurch*

Around the South Downs:
Midhurst
Hailsham

In Surrey:
Cranleigh
Gomshall*
Oxted*

In Kent:
Barham*
Borough Green*
Charing*
Hollingbourne*
Sandwich*
Sole Street*
Wye*

In the Weald of Sussex and Kent:
Balcombe*
Crowborough*
Heathfield
Midhurst
Wadhurst*

*Indicates a local train station

Chapter 2: Setting up, setting out and coming home

The Mountain Bike

Mountain Bikes (MTBs) are one of the most common types of bike in use today. Their main attraction is their versatility: they can be used for commuting, gentle family outings, exhilarating technical challenges and expeditions. They cost anything from £150– £3,000. The rides in this guide are suitable for an 'everyday' mountain bike.

1 Tough frames made from high tensile steel tubing – cromoly tubing is good because it is very strong, relatively light and inexpensive.

2 Saddle – there are two types, shown here is a micro-adjusting saddle for finer position adjustment. The clip type is also commonly used. Most saddles are designed for men and can be extremely uncomfortable on the female form. Women are advised to invest in a saddle designed for them.

3 Wide alloy rims are better than steel, they are easier to straighten, lighter, and provide better braking performance in the wet.

4 There are many types of tyres for MTBs – fat tyres with deep treads are good for mixed on and off-road cycling; thinner, shallow tread tyres are better for road riding.

5 Flat handlebars for an upright riding position.

6 Bar ends provide an extra hand position, useful for easier climbing and cruising on the flat.

7 Derailleur gears – fitted on all MTBs and provide 10-24 gears. The average MTB has 15-18 speeds which is sufficient for easy and medium grade rides. A minimum of 21 gears is necessary for tough off-road routes.

8 Gear shifters – there are four types; Shimano Rapidfire, thumb shifters, grip shifters and down type shifters for road bikes. The most common are rapidfire (shown here) and grip shifters.

9 Grips.

10 Indexed gears – mounted on the handlebar for accessible operation, the gear lever provides an audible and tactile click to indicate a gear change. Some bikes have a switch which disables the indexing.

11 Cantilever brakes – more powerful than traditional caliper brakes and essential for stopping quickly.

Sizing up

When buying a new or second-hand bike it is important to get one that is the correct size. Too big or too small and you could end up with numerous aches and strains. Follow the guidelines below and you should end up with a bike that is suited to your height and frame and is enjoyable to ride.

Sizing

There should be 7-10 cms (3-4 inches) between you and the cross bar when standing astride the bike – this is important if you have to jump off quickly.

Heading

SADDLE HEIGHT – adjust the saddle so that your hips don't rock when pedalling. When the ball of the foot is resting on the pedal, at the bottom of the rotation, the knee should be slightly bent.

◄ POSITION – adjust back or forward so that when the knee is flexed at 45 degrees, the knee and pedal axle are in a straight line.

ANGLE – experiment for a comfortable position.

Handlebars

Height – there is no right or wrong height, adjust for a comfortable fit.

◀ Reach – a good guide is to ensure that your back is at 45 degrees when in a natural riding position, but experiment for personal preference.

Sizing children's bikes

Kids love riding bikes. Mountain bikes are perfect because they get them off the streets and out of the way of traffic. There are many different grades of tracks that are suitable for children to ride on with their parents, a number of which are featured in Chapter 3. Good children's mountain bikes that offer the same sort of features as adult bikes are now available.

Sizing a mountain bike for a child is the same as for an adult. It may be tempting to buy a larger size so that it lasts longer but this is not a good idea because a child will have less control over the bike and may lose confidence.

Good-fitting helmets are particularly important for children (*see* pp 30-31, Essential accessories). Deck your child out with a full complement of reflectors (*see* pp 46-47, Safety and emergency).

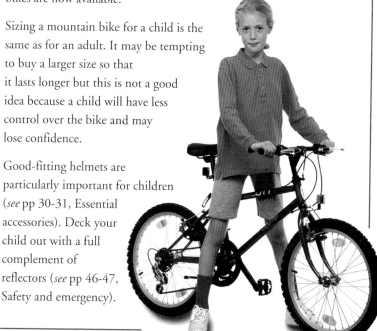

Essential accessories

Helmet – always wear a helmet, they can limit damage to one of the most vulnerable parts of the body. A good fit is essential, they should be snug and move with the scalp if you wiggle your eyebrows but not tight enough to pinch the sides of your head. A helmet that does not fit will not offer adequate protection.

Make sure a new helmet conforms to one of the following standards: Snell, ANSI, Eu, and BSI.

If you do have an accident, take the helmet back to the shop that sold it to you for checking. Helmets are designed to withstand one crash and damage is not always apparent to the eye.

Children's helmets

A child's head is especially vulnerable. Get children, and reluctant teenagers, into the habit of wearing a helmet from the start.

Remember

- don't buy a helmet for a child to grow into, a good fit is important
- make sure the helmet sits low enough on the head but has little side to side movement
- ensure the strap is adjusted so that the helmet cannot move
- avoid pinching a child's neck in the snap lock buckle, it is painful. Ask them to hold their chin up
- buy a helmet with some reflective material on the outer shell

Not essential but fun

A bike computer: they are useful for seeing how far you have gone and can tell you your maximum speed, average speed, total accumulated mileage and the time. Most have seven functions and are waterproof.

Tool kit 4, 5, and 6mm allen keys, multi tool (a selection of tools in a penknife format), small pliers, chain rivet extractor, chain ring bolt, spare chain links.

Puncture repair kit

Spare inner tube

Pump

Reflective belt in case you run out of daylight or the weather changes dramatically.

Map this guide uses Ordnance Survey Landranger 1:50,000. You are advised to buy the relevant map(s) for your route and not rely on the maps reproduced in this guide.

Compass

Oil in a small tin or grease in a packet.

Water bottle they vary in size from 0.75 litres to 1.5 litres.

Money and small change or a phone card for emergencies.

A watch to ensure you start the return journey in good time.

Lights necessary even if you don't expect to be riding in the dusk or dark. You may get delayed. LED lights are compact, light and have a 3-4 month battery life.

Bumbag for carrying money and valuables.

Panniers for carrying food and spare clothing.

Clothing for all weathers

There is a lot of specialist cycling gear in bike shops and the range can be rather daunting to an occasional or novice cyclist. Most people cannot go out and buy the complete outfit in one go and will have to make do with what is in the wardrobe with perhaps one or two specialist items. Here are some general guidelines to cope with the vagaries of the British weather and help make your ride as comfortable as possible.

- Wear loose clothing that allows complete freedom of movement.
- Choose materials such as cotton or Lycra mixes which can breathe.
- If you buy one item of cycling gear, make it a pair of padded cycling shorts, they provide comfort from the saddle and are designed not to chafe the skin.

Being properly dressed for bad weather and good (below) makes riding enjoyable

- Wear a top that does not expose areas of skin, particularly the bottom of the back and the lower arms.
- Wear, or pack, several layers of clothing so that you can shed or add as the temperature changes.
- Make sure the layer closest to your skin is made of a material that can breathe.
- Always take a waterproof; cycling in cold wet clothes is miserable.
- Use glasses to protect your eyes from dust, insects and bright sunshine. Specialist cycling glasses (above right) are designed for that purpose.
- Gloves can stop you shredding your hands if you come off the bike and padded ones provide some shock absorption.
- It is not essential to buy cycling shoes, although if you intend to cycle very regularly it might be a good idea. Tennis shoes and trainers are good substitutes.

Fine weather essentials

- sunglasses
- sun cream
- long sleeved top in case it gets chilly

specialist glasses protect the eyes and are less likely to break

A long sleeved top for riding off-road.

Foul weather essentials

- hat
- scarf
- thermal top and bottom
- several long-sleeved tops for layering
- waterproof boots
- waterproof gloves
- A thermal layer next to the skin in wet or cold conditions maintains core warmth (chest and back)
- A balaclava keeps head and ears warm when it is cold
- Two pairs of gloves and socks keep extremities from getting icy in winter

Wash padded cycling shorts after every ride to keep them in good condition

Tips

- Legs and arms can get scratched when riding off-road, long sleeves and trousers may be more appropriate
- Keep spare clothes in the car – muddy clothes do not mix well with the insides of pubs and tearooms
- Keep a black bin liner in the car for wet and muddy clothes

padded gloves

Food and drink

Your body uses a lot of energy when cycling, particularly on tougher rides, so it is very important to carry food and drink with you, even on the shortest rides. If you rely on the pub or teashop they will inevitably be closed. And if you get delayed by a mechanical fault or an injury, it could be some time before you get to the next watering hole.

The golden rules are to eat before you are hungry and drink before you are thirsty. It is a good idea to find some shelter when you stop for refreshment to avoid getting chilled, particularly in exposed areas of the country. A hollow in the ground will do.

Please remember to take all litter with you when you have finished your snack. Litter can be a major hazard to wildlife and spoils the countryside for other people.

Flapjacks are a favourite mountain biker's snack

Remember to eat before you are hungry

Food

Snacking is better than having one big meal. Complex carbohydrates are the best energy givers. They take longer to digest and release their nutrients at a steady rate. Chocolate and sweet snacks give an immediate energy boost which fades rapidly. Flapjacks, malt loaf, dried fruit, nuts and bananas are all nutritious and easy to carry. Specialist cycling food is sometimes overhyped and overpriced but may be worth a try.

Complex carbohydrates such as bananas, dried fruit and nuts provide energy while you are on the trail

Drink

Water is by far the best drink to carry with you because it is easily absorbed by the body. Dehydration can happen quickly, particularly on long rides in hot weather, therefore aim to drink every 20-30 minutes. Don't underestimate how much water your body can lose on a hard trip, even in winter. Carry some extra water in the car. Don't drink from a stream unless you are sure it is close to a good spring. Avoid sweet and fizzy drinks.

Tip

Clear water bottles help you see if the bottle has gone mouldy and tell you how much is in there.

Preparing your bike

Before you start out on a journey it is good to get into the habit of a pre-ride check. If you are not confident about doing it yourself, many shops will oblige for a small fee. However, the steps below are fairly easy to accomplish and give you the best chance of a trouble-free ride.

1 ► Ensure that all the bolts on the bike are tight.

2 Run through the gears and ensure that the changes are crisp.

3 Look for damaged or stiff links in the chain: spinning the cranks backwards should show you if there is a problem because the chain will jump.

4 Check there is enough lubrication on the chain.

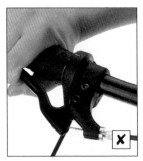

5 Pull on the brake lever, if it moves easily a long way towards the handlebar, the brakes need adjusting.

6 Worn brake blocks will not do their job. Replace them when it becomes necessary.

7 All the strands on a cable should be twisted together. Frayed or rusty brake cable must be replaced immediately.

8 Inspect tyres for flints and thorns, gouges from brake blocks and general wear. Worn or damaged tyres are more prone to puncture.

9 Measure the tyre pressure with a pressure gauge. You will find the recommended pressure marked on the sides of the tyre.

If you don't have a gauge, squeeze the tyre sides: you should be able to push your thumb about a ½ cm (¼ inch) into a correctly inflated mountain bike tyre.

Ensure tyres are well inflated for off-road surfaces where punctures are more likely.

10 ▶ Spin the wheels to check if they are straight, using the brake blocks as a guide. Listen for scuffing noises which indicate a dent. Small dents can be hammered out with a rubber mallet, larger ones mean the wheels need replacing.

11 Look for bent and damaged spokes.

Transporting your bike

A lot of people live in cities and cities tend to be a long way from areas where people want to ride their mountain bikes. It is possible to get to the start of some of the routes in this book by train. However, the most usual method of transporting your bike is on, in or behind the car.

By car

Roof racks, boot racks and tow bar racks are the alternatives to bagging (see box) when transporting your bike by car, although just removing the wheels and saddle may be enough to fit a small bike or bikes into a large car. Secure fixing and regular checking is of the utmost importance whichever of the options you choose.

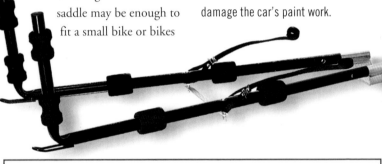

Tow bar racks are secure and won't damage the car's paint work.

Be legal

Boot and tow bar racks cover up your rear tail lights and number plate. You must use a tow plate with your number plate attached so that other road users can clearly see your brakes and number plate. Many police forces are vigilant about this and may take action if you are in breach of the law.

Bagging your bike

Dismantling your bike and carrying it in a bag is a good way of getting round reluctant train and coach operators and also transporting your bike inside your car. It is important to pad the tubing and wheel to prevent scratches and knocks. It is also essential to double check that you have put all the components into the bag along with the tools needed for reassembly at your destination.

Boot and roof racks

Boot racks are becoming one of the most popular ways of transporting bikes. Up to 99 per cent of cars can be fitted with a boot rack: they are easy to attach and relatively cheap. Most are designed to carry up to three bikes. Roof rack manufacturers offer fitting kits to allow you to carry anything from skis to canoes, including bikes. They can be carried upside down, upright and with the front wheel removed. See the box opposite to ensure you are travelling legally.

Tow bar racks

These can save damage to the body work of your car and are as strong and secure as a boot rack.

By train

Most rail networks will let you take your bike onto their trains. However, policy varies from region to region and country to country so always check before arriving at the station.

By coach and bus

Coach and bus companies have their own policies on transporting bikes, so check in advance that you will be allowed on.

By air

Most major airlines will carry your bike. Check with the airline when you book your tickets. Your bike will have to be boxed up or bagged (*see* above).

Preparing yourself: stretching

Cycling is good exercise and an excellent way of keeping in shape. Like all forms of exercise, you are far less likely to get an injury if you make sure your muscles are warmed up before you start. Simple stretches will greatly improve your flexibility and endurance. The following steps should take 5-10 minutes.

Back

Sit on the floor with your legs stretched out in front of you. Bend your body forwards from the waist/hip aiming to put your nose on your knees. It doesn't matter if you can bend just a couple of inches or all the way. Stop as soon as it hurts.

Legs

Your legs are going to work hardest of all, particularly on a long ride with several climbs. These three exercises will prepare you for what is to come.

◀ Stretch the calf muscles by extending one leg straight behind you, foot flat on the floor, and holding the stretch for 30 seconds. Move your rear foot further back and hold this for 30 seconds. Repeat with the other leg.

Shoulder

Clasp your hands together behind you by reaching your left hand over your shoulder so that your right elbow is pointing straight up and your left hand up behind the back. Hold the position for 30 seconds. Repeat, reversing the position of the arms.

Neck

Stand relaxed and turn your head from left to right slowly, holding it for at least 30 seconds at the farthest reach each side. Then gently raise and lower your chin.

Groin

Sit on the floor with your legs apart at 45 degrees or as far as they will go. With both hands, reach towards the right foot and hold the position for 30 seconds. Repeat to the left.

◄ Stand on one leg and bring the knee of your other leg up towards your chin. Clasp your hands together around the raised leg and pull it up to your chest, keeping your back straight. Hold the position for 30 seconds. Repeat with the other leg.

▶ To stretch the hamstring, cross one leg in front of the other, keeping your feet close together. Gently bend forwards as far as you can go from the waist/hip, keeping your back straight. Hold this position for 30 seconds. Repeat, crossing the other leg in front.

41

On the trail

When out riding, remember that there are other people using the trails for their own enjoyment. Polite, helpful and considerate conduct is important so that mountain bikers are not seen as a menace by the rest of the population. Following the MTB code below will make you a good ambassador for all mountain bikers.

MTB code

1 Give way to other trail users.
2 Always be courteous to other trail users.
3 Take every bit of rubbish away with you.
4 Leave gates as you find them.
5 Never skid, especially on wet soft ground (to avoid erosion).
6 Ride with respect for your surroundings.
7 Check that you have legal access to the land you are on.
8 Always take note of MOD flagpoles.
9 Warn horses and walkers of your approach by ringing your bell, singing, whistling or talking to your cycle partners.

Courtesy to other trail users costs nothing and enhances the reputation of mountain biking

Below are a few tips to make your life easier and safer out on the trail.

- Plan your ride with the weakest member of your group in mind.
- Let the slowest rider set the pace.
- Off-road, leave a reasonable distance between you and the rider in front.
- The deepest part of a puddle is where vehicle wheels go; try the middle higher ground.
- Anticipate hills; change to the right gear in good time.
- On-road, help weaker riders by getting them to ride in your slipstream.
- Remove vegetation from derailleurs (gears) immediately to prevent against damage.
- Faster riders should go ahead and open and close gates for the rest of the group to balance the differences in strength.
- Keep money and keys with you at all times, even if you leave other gear on the bike.
- Fold your map to the section you need in the dry and out of the wind.

Mountain bikers have to share many trails with other users

Navigation

It is easy to get lost while mountain biking. A combination of tight twisty trails and changing scenery makes it easy to become disorientated and lose your sense of direction. Routes also look different according to the time of year.

A LWAYS CARRY a map of the area. You will find the number and name of the map for each ride in this guide in the ride specification box. Observation is the key to successful navigation in unknown territory. Make a mental note of distinctive features such as steep contours, rivers, forested areas and tracks before you begin and look for them on route.

If you become lost, stay in a group and work together to find your way home. Don't separate; both parties may end up lost! Retrace your steps to a point where you know where you are. If necessary go back to the start the way you came. Try to rejoin the route at a later stage or find a road alternative on the map. If you can't do this, stop at the next signpost or landmark, consult your map and take a compass bearing.

Checking the map to decide in which direction to continue

Taking a compass bearing

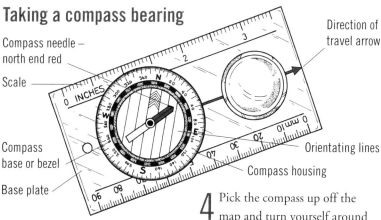

- Compass needle – north end red
- Scale
- Compass base or bezel
- Base plate
- Direction of travel arrow
- Orientating lines
- Compass housing

A compass becomes essential once you are lost and is always useful in forestry areas. The illustration above shows the most useful type of compass which usually comes with instructions. The following steps will help you determine in which direction to travel according to the route on your map.

1 Roughly orientate the map so the north edge is facing north.

2 Place the compass flat on the map with the long edge of the baseplate along the desired direction of travel. In other words either connecting, or in line with, where you are currently standing and the next point on the route.

3 Rotate the capsule until the N on the compass dial or bezel, not the needle, points to North on the map. You have now taken a bearing.

4 Pick the compass up off the map and turn yourself around until the red end of the needle points to N on the compass dial and lines up with the orientating lines in the base of the dial. The large 'direction of travel' arrow will now point precisely at your destination.

5 Choose a landmark on this line of travel and ride towards it without looking at the compass: there is no need and minor curves and deviations in the track will only confuse the issue.

6 When you reach this first landmark repeat the procedure until you reach your destination.

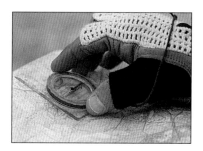

Safety and emergency

Safety is, of course, a priority – particularly if you are riding with children. There is a lot that common sense will tell you. However, a few reminders are always useful.

Safety precautions

- Always wear a helmet, even on the shortest route. You can never predict what other track and road users are going to do. The one time you go out without your helmet on is the time you will most need it. Nothing can prevent the damage that a car speeding at 60mph causes, but protecting your head can limit injury in lot of instances.
- Take great care crossing roads, particularly main A roads. Dismount, and use a pedestrian crossing if there is one. Read ahead in the ride directions to alert yourself to road crossings and warn others in your group, especially children, that a road is coming up.
- Avoid riding on busy roads with young children and inexperienced riders. Try to find a quieter alternative.
- If you are riding in poor light or at night, make sure your lights are on and that you are wearing some reflective clothing. Ankle bands are particularly good at alerting car drivers to your presence. Also, kit your children out with the full range of reflectors.
- Check the local weather forecast before you embark on a ride, particularly if you intend to be out for a long time. Try to make a educated guess as to whether it is riding weather.
- Tell someone where you are going and, if possible, leave a marked up map of the area at home. It will help locate you in the event of a rescue team being called out.
- Take adequate supplies of food and drink to prevent against dehydration. Don't be over ambitious. Choose a ride well within your capabilities or you might find yourself in trouble in the middle of a route.

What to do in emergencies

Due to the nature of off-road riding it is quite possible that you may have to deal with an accident involving another rider. There are several things to remember:

- Place the rider in the recovery position using the minimum of movement (see First aid pp48-49). Keep the rider warm and place a jacket underneath their head for comfort
- If they have sustained a head injury do not remove their helmet unless they are bleeding severely
- Do not give food in case they need to be operated on in a hurry
- If you have to leave an injured rider to seek assistance make sure that they are warm and feel able to stay awake
- Make a note of where you have left them on your map and mark the spot with a piece of bright clothing held down by a stone or attached to a tree
- Get help as quickly as possible

Keep an accident victim warm and get help as soon as possible

47

First Aid

Every mountain biker, indeed every cyclist, comes off their bike sooner or later. It is a good idea to carry a small first aid kit with you on trips to cope with cut and bruises.

When a person is seriously injured the priority is to ring 999 and get an ambulance to them as quickly as possible. Describe your location as accurately as you can. It is useful to be able to tell the emergency services as much as possible about the accident and the state of the patient when they arrive.

Minor injuries

- Small cuts and grazes can be rinsed with cold water from a drinking bottle. Apply some antiseptic and cover with a clean plaster.

- Dizziness and faintness might occur after a crash or spill. Sit down comfortably until the feeling passes. If it doesn't improve place the head between the knees.

Simple first aid kit

- As a minimum, take the following: water bottle, antiseptic lotion or cream, plasters, cottonwool.

Major injuries

- If someone has a serious crash or spill remaining calm is vital. You cannot help another person if you are in a panic. Don't expect too much of yourself: you may be suffering from shock as well as the injured party.

- Assess the situation. Stop the traffic if it may be a danger to the injured person and try to enlist the help of a third party.

- Assess the injured. Are they conscious? If they are, ask them how they feel and if they can describe their injuries.

- Bleeding needs to be stopped. If possible raise the wound and apply a compress firmly over the bleeding area until it ceases.

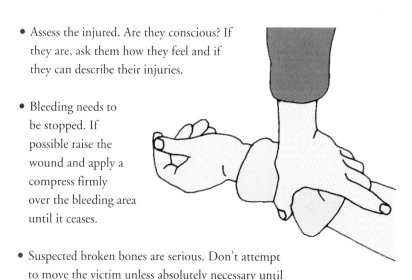

- Suspected broken bones are serious. Don't attempt to move the victim unless absolutely necessary until professional help arrives.

- Check for a pulse by placing your fingers on the victim's voice box. If there is no pulse and their breathing has stopped you could try resuscitation – however, only do so if you know how.

- Keep the injured person warm, offer reassuring words and hold their hand until help arrives. Don't give them food or drink in case they need an emergency operation.

- If you are sure the injured person does not have a spinal injury, place them in the recovery position.

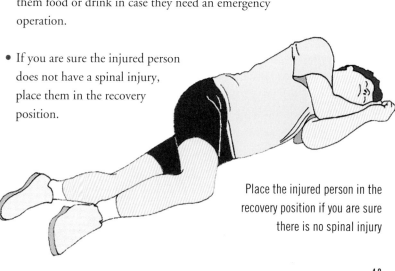

Place the injured person in the recovery position if you are sure there is no spinal injury

When you get home

Cleaning the bike after a ride is a job most people hate and would skip if they had any choice. However, it is essential if you want to maximise the life of your bike and ensure it is always in good working order. The following is a six step procedure which should take about 10 minutes.

Tools

Ideally use a hose with a brush head and soap reservoir, car shampoo and WD40 for lubrication. Keep high pressure water spraying away from the bearings in case the seals cannot withstand a strong jet of water.

1 Hose off the worst of the mud while it is still wet.

2 Use a hose brush head (or a brush and hose) to scrub off any lumps of mud and finish the initial rinse.

3 Using car shampoo, gently scrub off remaining dirt with soapy water.

4 Rinse off the soap with plain water and repeat the shampoo and rinse if necessary.

5 Use degreaser on ground-in dirt and rinse off with plain water.

6 Let the water drip off and spray exposed metal or moving parts with WD40.

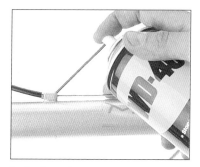

Lubrication

WD40 is an adequate and relatively cheap oil for general lubrication. Apply it immediately after cleaning to:

1 rear brake pivots
2 rear mech pivot points
3 rear mech jockey wheels
4 front mech points

5 brake lever pivots
6 front brake pivots
7 cable ends at the stops

Use a heavier oil such as standard mineral-based medium weight oil for the chain.

Chapter 3: The rides

1 Appledore

The landscape around Appledore is composed of rich arable land and pasture, more like East Anglia than the traditional view of Kent. Ideal for families, this route explores a network of virtually traffic-free lanes with no hills to worry about.

GRADE easy	
DISTANCE 26 kms (16 miles)	
TIME allow 2.5 hours	
MAP OS Landranger 189 Ashford and Romney Marsh	
GRID REF AT START 957292	
PARKING main street in Appledore	
TRAINS nearest station Appledore	
TERRAIN flat, open arable and pasture land	
SEASONAL SUITABILITY all year	
SURFACE tarmac	
CLIMBS/DESCENTS n/a	
REFRESHMENTS tearooms, Red Lion PH, Swan PH, Appledore; Woolpack PH, Royal Oak PH, Brookland; The Bell PH, Ivychurch; Red Lion PH, Snargate	

1 Start in Appledore with your back to the Red Lion PH. Turn left, go straight ahead through the traffic lights, over the bridge and turn first right alongside the canal. Continue for 5.5 kms (3.25 miles).

2 Ignore the first left. Shortly after Puddock Farm on the right, turn next left by a triangle of grass signposted 'Brookland, New Romney'.

3 Take the second left shortly after a line of tall evergreen trees. Continue for 1.6 kms (1 mile).

4 In Brookland at the offset crossroads with the A259 go straight ahead onto Boarmans Lane. Take care on a sharp left-hand bend and bear right signposted 'Post Office'. Follow for 2 kms (1.25 miles).

5 Ignore two left turns at railway crossings, take the third left. Continue for 2.5 kms (1.5 miles). Shortly after passing Coldharbour Farm, take first left on a sharp right-hand bend.

6 At the crossroads with the A259, a red brick bungalow opposite, go straight ahead. Continue for 2.5 kms (1.5 miles).

7 At the T-junction in Ivychurch, turn left (turn right for the The Bell PH). Continue for 1.6kms (1 mile).

8 Just before a grey corrugated metal barn turn right onto a narrower lane. After 1.2.kms (0.75 miles) turn first left.

9 At T-junction with A2070 turn right then left. Continue for 2.5 kms (1.5 miles).

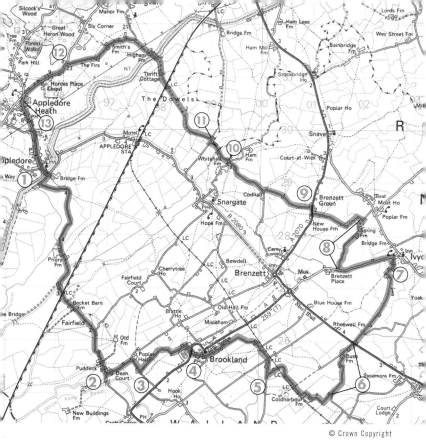

10 At crossroads go straight ahead signposted 'Warehorne, Snargate'.

11 Go over a red brick bridge, turn right at T-junction signposted 'Warehorne' then first left. Continue for 5 kms (3 miles) passing over the old Military Canal.

12 At the T-junction with a wider road turn left.

13 At the crossroads in Appledore Heath by a telephone box turn left signposted 'Appledore ¾' to return to the start. This final section may be a little busier than the rest.

May blossom near Snargate

2 The Meon Valley

This ride takes you along the quietest and most rural of the dismantled railway paths in the southeast. Enjoy long stretches beneath a green panoply of over-arching trees and a spring carpet of bluebells near Wickham on a route which can be any length up to 32 kms (20 miles).

The route is linear and does not need much direction. If you are pedalling north from Wickham in the direction of Droxford, you are at Droxford when you come to a short tarmac stretch. To get off the path here, bear left over the wooden barrier and left again at the T-junction with the road for Droxford. Turn right at the T-junction with the road and go under the railway bridge for The Hurdles pub. The section between West Meon and Droxford is a little rougher than the section to the south where the surface is smoother and suitable all year round.

GRADE	easy
DISTANCE	up to 32 kms (20 miles)
TIME	allow 3.5 hours
MAP	OS Landranger 196 Solent and the Isle of Wight and 185 Winchester and Basingstoke
GRID REF AT START	643236 (West Meon) or 613206 (Droxford) or 576117 (Wickham)
PARKING	see below
TRAINS	nearest stations Botley, Fareham
TERRAIN	wooded cuttings and embankments through farmland
SEASONAL SUITABILITY	south of Droxford all year, Droxford to West Meon late spring to late autumn
SURFACE	stone-based tracks best section Droxford to Wickham
CLIMBS/DESCENTS	n/a
REFRESHMENTS	teashops and pubs in Wickham; White Horse PH ,The Hurdles PH, Droxford; Red Lion PH, Thomas Lord PH, West Meon

1 West Meon: heading south through West Meon on the A32, take first left after the Red Lion PH into Station Road. After the end of the flint wall on the left bear right, uphill, on a tarmac track. Parking is at the top, beware of the height barrier.

2 Droxford: park in centre of village near the telephone box or by the Post Office. For the railway path go along Mill Lane (No Through Road) past the houses, alongside the stream then across the bridge. At the B2150 turn right and right again 50m (55 yards) before the railway bridge by a '4.5 mts height limit' sign. At the cycle path turn right for Wickham (better surface) or left for West Meon (becomes rougher).

3 To get to the car park, from the main square in Wickham, follow signs for 'free car park' on the road that swings right past the White Lion PH. Soon after the pub turn left on to Mill Lane then right on to Station Close (No Through Road) and right again into the carpark. The railway path starts here.

3 Along the Cuckoo Trail

This railway path in the heart of Sussex was named after the tradition of releasing the first cuckoo of spring at Heathfield Fair each year.

GRADE	easy

GRADE easy

DISTANCE up to 35.5 kms (22 miles)

TIME allow 3.5 hours

MAP OS Landranger 199 Eastbourne and Hastings

GRID REF AT START 584051 (Polegate) 589093 (Hailsham) 581214 (Heathfield)

PARKING Polegate: turn left off the A27 as you head east through Polegate into School Lane, then left into Windsor Way, park near the library or community centre. Hailsham: from town centre, follow signs for Eastbourne A295 onto South Road. Just past Hailsham Free Church, take next left for parking. Heathfield: opposite Barclays Bank in High Street, turn into Station Road, then second right, Newnham Way and immediately left for parking

TRAINS Polegate railway station

TERRAIN relatively flat

SEASONAL SUITABILITY all year

SURFACE good: tarmac or aggregate

CLIMBS/DESCENTS slow gentle climb from Polegate to Hailsham

REFRESHMENTS plenty of choice in the three main towns

1 The trail starts in School Lane, Polegate, which is left off the A27 as you head east through the town. The start is 180 m (200 yds) on the right. Head north for 5.5 kms (3.5 miles) to the outskirts of Hailsham.

2 Just outside Hailsham, follow the signs for the Cuckoo Trail which take you along Freshfield Close. At the end of this road, turn right into Lindfield Drive. This ends at a T-junction with the A295 and with a pond in front of you. Turn left, go 275m (300 yds). If you use the wide pavement to the left of the road dismount and walk.

3 Pass the Railway Tavern on your right and turn left into the carpark. Cross the carpark diagonally, under the bridge and continue on the trail towards Heathfield 12 kms (7.5 miles) further on.

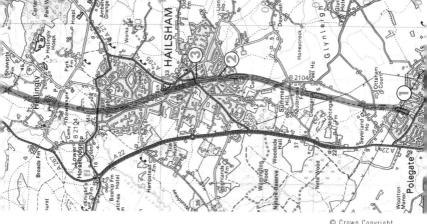

4 The trail ends in a small gravel carpark at Heathfield. If you want to go into the centre of Heathfield, turn right at the end of the carpark and left uphill, at the next T-junction. Or turn round and follow the trail back to Polegate. From this direction there are good views of the South Downs as you approach Polegate.

A metalwork sculpture on the Cuckoo Trail

4 The Basingstoke Canal

One of the best canal towpaths in the south, this broad, stone-based track is easily tackled by younger cyclists. There is a traffic-free route from Putney Bridge to Odiham, a distance of over 80.5 kms (50 miles) via the Thames Towpath and the whole length of the Basingstoke Canal.

GRADE easy

DISTANCE 14.5 kms (9 miles)

TIME allow 2 hours

MAP OS Landranger 186 Aldershot and Guildford

GRID REF AT START 894552

PARKING Basingstoke Canal Centre, Mytchett. On A331 (A321) follow signs for Mytchett and brown signs for Canal Centre

TRAINS nearest stations Ash Vale and Brookwood. Stations along the length of the canal

TERRAIN good, well-drained stone base. Surrey section is better than Hampshire section. The boundary is just west of Ash

SEASONAL SUITABILITY all year

CLIMBS/DESCENTS n/a

REFRESHMENTS teashop, Canal Centre; Potters PH near start; Kings Head PH, crossing with the B3012; Lock Cottage teashop, Lock 28 (Sundays and Bank Holiday Mondays open 2-6pm)

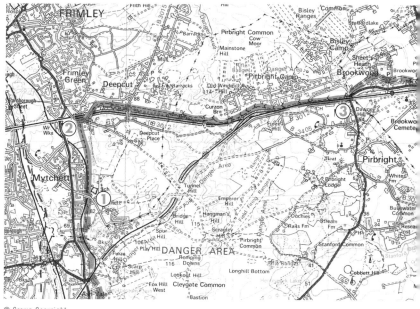

© Crown Copyright

1 Start at the Canal Centre, return to the road, turn right over the bridge then right along the canal towpath. Continue for 1.6 kms (1 mile).

2 After crossing the B3012, the towpath changes sides and passes alongside a series of 14 locks which comprise Deepcut Flight. Continue for 5.5 kms (3.5 miles).

3 At the new red-brick bridge at Pirbright Lock (No. 15) turn round and return to the start. Continue on towards London if you wish! The towpath frequently changes sides.

One of the 14 locks that make up Deepcut Flight

5 Downs Link one

As its name suggests, the Downs Link is a north-south route linking the North Downs Way and the South Downs Way, the two premier long-distance trails in the southeast of the country. Two rides use this 'highway' (*see* map right). The first is a short jaunt between Bramley and Cranleigh with the option to go further south as far as Slinfold through the delightful wood south of the Thurlow Arms.

GRADE easy

DISTANCE 8 kms (5 miles) or more

TIME allow 2 hours

MAP OS Landranger 186 Aldershot and Guildford and 187 Dorking, Reigate and Crawley

GRID REF AT START 009451 (Bramley)

PARKING Bramley and Wonersh old station carpark. At junction of A281 and B2128, take exit at mini roundabout 'Wonersh, Shamley Green'. After 180 m (200 yds) turn left signposted 'Bramley Business Centre. Bramley and Wonersh Railway Station'

TRAINS nearest station Shalford nr Bramley

TERRAIN embankments and cuttings through woodland

SEASONAL SUITABILITY all year

SURFACE good stone-based, rough section

CLIMBS/DESCENTS 1 climb

REFRESHMENTS teashops and pubs in Cranleigh and Bramley

Easy cycling on the Downs Link

1 Start at Bramley and Wonersh old station carpark. Return to the road and go diagonally left across the road to the bridlegate signposted 'No motorcycles'. Continue for 8 kms (5 miles) to Cranleigh.

2 If you want to continue along the railway path which has a good surface for many miles, in Cranleigh go straight across the road towards the houses and follow signs for 'Downs Link' on the track running between playing fields.

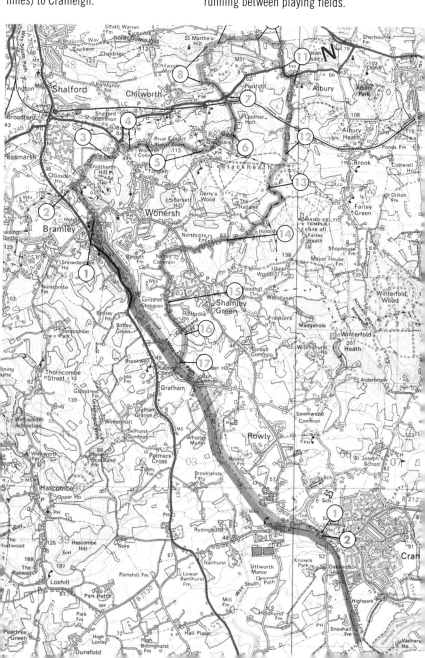

6 Downs Link two

The second ride is lollipop shaped incorporating some rough sections and parts where the underlying sand makes the going very slow. The views and the woodland justify the effort.

GRADE medium/hard

DISTANCE 30.5 kms (19 miles)

TIME allow 3.5 hours

MAP OS Landranger 186 Aldershot and Guildford and 187 Dorking, Reigate and Crawley

GRID REF AT START 055393

PARKING main carpark in Cranleigh off the High Street B2128 near the NatWest Bank

TERRAIN embankments and cuttings, sandy woodland and arable farmland

SEASONAL SUITABILITY all year 1–2, late autumn to late spring 2–17

SURFACE firm aggregate to sandy tracks and woodland

CLIMBS/DESCENTS 2 climbs, 1 steep

REFRESHMENTS teashops and pubs in Cranleigh, Bramley, Wonersh, Chilworth and Shamley Green; Drummond Arms, Albury

1 Start at the main carpark in Cranleigh. Exit at the far corner and turn right onto the Downs Link for 8 kms (5 miles). At the junction with the B2128 in Bramley, go straight across for 1.2 kms (0.75 miles).

2 At the red-brick bridge turn right and join the road. At the T-junction at the end of Tannery Lane go straight ahead onto the track past a house called Southlands. There are muddy sections on this narrow, climbing track.

3 Turn left at the T-junction of tracks in the direction signposted

'Bridleway' –' The Tower' is signposted right – onto another muddy section.

4 At the main road go straight ahead signposted 'Downs Link' onto a rough section. At T-junction with a minor lane turn left. At a fork of tracks by an old brick and timber house bear slightly right uphill.

5 Go straight on at a crossroads of tracks by a house. The surface becomes sandy. At the next junction with a road go straight ahead – 'Blackheath' is signposted right – onto a broad track, then shortly turn right, following the 'Downs Link' signs.

6 Follow blue waymarks through the sandy pine wood and onto the track to the right of the wooden fence alongside Lingwood House.

7 Cross the bridge over the railway. At the crossroads with A248 go straight on towards the church on the horizon.

8 Cross the stream, go past some houses on the right and take the first track right uphill signposted 'Downs Link'. The steep climb becomes a sandy push. At the junction of tracks by a Downs Link noticeboard and wooden

The view from St Martha's Hill

signpost bear right past the concrete pill box. (Please walk to visit the church as this is a footpath not a bridleway).

9 After a descent for 365 m (400 yds), at a three-way junction take the left-hand track through the carpark. At the road turn right then take the first track left between fences, signposted 'Bridleway' – it may be rough.

10 At a crossroads of tracks, with a red-tile farm on the left, go straight ahead through a bridlegate and bear diagonally right across the field, through a metal gate and turn left through a wooden bridlegate for a short, steep descent. At the T-junction with a major track turn right downhill.

11 Turn left at the T junction with the A248, at the end of Water Lane, into Albury. Then take the first road right by a carved signpost 'To the church. No Through Road'. Shortly, on a sharp left-hand bend, bear right onto Blackheath Lane signposted 'Unsuitable for motor vehicles'.

12 Go up the sunken lane which soon becomes a track. At a fork of tracks, bear right onto the steeper, narrower track signposted 'Bridleway'. At a second fork of tracks bear right again following the blue arrow and bridleway signs.

13 After numerous crossroads of tracks emerge at a wooden bungalow and bear left. After 365 m (400 yds), at a junction by a triangle of grass, bear right.

14 At the T-junction at the end of Green Lane bear left signposted 'Shamley Green, Cranleigh'. Then, go straight ahead at the crossroads with the B2128, signposted 'Lordshill ¾'.

15 Shortly after passing houses and the village green, on a sharp left-hand bend by a triangle of grass, bear right (straight ahead) signposted 'Bridleway'.

16 After Long Common Cottage, the tarmac lane becomes a track. After 365m (400 yds) fork right and cross the wooden bridge over a stream.

17 Follow the obvious track around the edge of the first field, diagonally right across a second field, then at a T-junction with a major track bear left. Just before the bridge turn right downhill to rejoin the Downs Link. Turn left to return to Cranleigh.

7 Bedgebury

Together with King's Wood (*see* p 78) Bedgebury Forest represents the best of the easy forestry trails in Kent. The route starts at the Pinetum which houses a magnificent collection of conifers and brightly flowering shrubs. Glimpses of them on your ride may tempt you to visit properly.

GRADE easy/medium	
DISTANCE 19 kms (12 miles)	
TIME allow 2.5 hours	
MAP OS Landranger 188 Maidstone and the Weald of Kent	
GRID REF AT START 714337	
PARKING Bedgebury Pinetum carpark	
TRAINS nearest station Etchingham	
TERRAIN Forestry Commission land, hop plantations and arable land	
SEASONAL SUITABILITY late spring to late autumn	
SURFACE broad stone-based, 2 muddy sections	
CLIMBS/DESCENTS 2 climbs	
REFRESHMENTS shop at entrance to Bedgebury Pinetum; Wellington Arms off A229 north of Hawkhurst	

1 Start at Bedgebury Pinetum carpark. Turn right out of the carpark for 365m (400 yds) then take the first road right signposted 'Bridleway'. Continue for 0.8 kms (0.5 miles).

2 The tarmac lane turns to track shortly after the park office. Go straight ahead for 2 kms (1.25 miles).

3 Go past a house with tall brick chimneys (Louisa Lodge). The track turns to tarmac. At the top of a short hill turn right ★ onto a tarmac track signposted 'Tanyard Farm. Reserved rights'.

4 Follow this drive past hop plantations, through the farm and onto a narrower, grassy track, descending steeply. This is a short very rough section and is muddy in winter. Go down then up, keep bearing left on the main track which soon improves.

5 At the road turn right. At the T-junction with the A268, at the end of Slip Mill Lane, turn right then first left.

6 After 0.8 kms (0.5 miles) turn sharp right at the T-junction signposted 'Flimwell 2'. Go straight across the A268 onto the No Through Road signposted 'Bridleway'.

7 Soon the road swings right. Immediately after a cattle grid bear left downhill on a concrete track. Follow this to its end then bear right onto a stone track.

8 Follow the field edge around a sharp left-hand bend. On a sharp right-hand bend leave the main track and continue straight ahead on a narrow, rough, sometimes muddy track along the edge of woodland.

9 Climb on a broad earth track for 365m (400 yds) then take the first left downhill. At the T-junction with a major stone-based forestry track turn right. Then turn left at a crossroads of tracks. Continue for 1.6 kms (1 mile).

10 At the T-junction with wooden sheds turn right. Bear left at a fork of tracks by a large wooden shed with a corrugated roof. Follow this track past the mast for a fast downhill with good views. At the next fork bear left.

11 With a wooden gate ahead and the sign 'No horse riding, no cycling', follow the track around the edge of the Pinetum. Climb steadily. At the top, by a wooden post, turn sharp left at the T junction signposted 'Diverted bridleway'.

12 Go past the Pinetum on the left. At the T-junction, by some buildings, rejoin the outward route and turn left past the red brick Forestry Commission offices. At the road turn left to return to the carpark.

The Pinetum at Bedgebury Forest

★ A For a winter/wet weather alternative or a visit to the Wellington Arms PH, go straight ahead for 1.2 kms (0.75 miles) then turn sharply right on the first tarmac road. After 1.6 kms (1 mile) turn right at the T-junction. After 0.8 kms (0.5 miles) turn first left for the pub or continue straight to rejoin the main route at direction no.5.

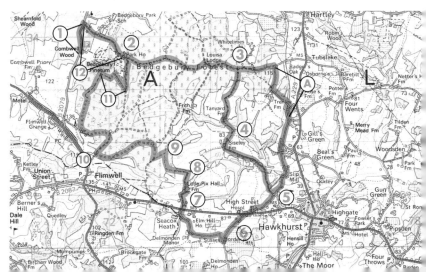

8 Around Bewl Water

Bewl Water is one of the largest reservoirs in the southeast with the potential to rival Grafham Water in Cambridgeshire and Derwent Water in the Peak District as a cycling facility. Round Reservoir Route signs as well as other people's cycle tracks help to identify the way. The surface can be very rough and is impassable in winter but on a fine summer's day you should have a most enjoyable trip.

GRADE	medium
DISTANCE	21 kms (13 miles)
TIME	allow 3.5 hours
MAP	OS Landranger 188 Maidstone and the Weald of Kent
GRID REF AT START	675338
PARKING	Bewl Water Visitor Centre off A21
TRAINS	Wadhurst station
TERRAIN	wooded slopes, open pasture
SEASONAL SUITABLITY	late spring to late autumn. Avoid after prolonged rain even in summer
SURFACE	some aggregate, mainly clay base which is hard going
CLIMBS/DESCENTS	2 road climbs
REFRESHMENTS	teas at start; Bull Inn, Three Leg Cross

1 From the carpark make your way down to the dam which has footpath status so you must take the track below the dam and rejoin the trail at its far end.

2 Immediately after crossing the dam, the route enters woodland.

3 The trail briefly joins a minor lane to cross the eastern-most creek of the reservoir. This is followed by a 3 km (2-mile) section of woodland mixed with pasture.

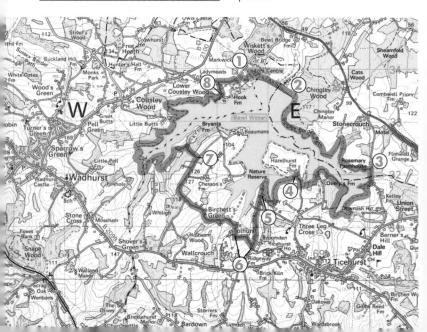

4 At Hazelhurst Farm the bridleway runs to the left of and parallel to the farm drive.

5 The trail climbs on tarmac lanes away from the lake at its southern tip for 1.6 kms (1 mile). (If you wish to visit the Bull PH at Three Leg Cross, take the first road left as you climb on tarmac by a triangle of grass and a house called 'Rowley'.)

Buttercups at Bewl Water

6 At the top of the climb take an easily missed right turn, by a small letter box. Then at the fork of lanes bear right (not Quarry Farm).

7 The trail leaves the tarmac lanes and returns to the lakeside. This section through Cousley Wood is one of the roughest parts of the ride.

8 A final climb away from the reservoir takes you to the lane that leads back to the Visitor Centre.

9 Trottiscliffe and Coldrum Long Barrow

The wooded slopes of the North Downs changed dramatically in October 1987 when the 'Great Gale' roared through, knocking down thousands of trees. This route along the North Downs way starts at the snall village of Trottiscliffe and takes you past the standing stones of Coldrum Long Barrow, a Neolithic burial ground.

GRADE	medium
DISTANCE	14.5 kms (9 miles)
TIME	allow 1.5 hours
MAP	OS Landranger 188 Maidstone and the Weald of Kent
GRID REF AT START	643603
PARKING	village hall carpark, Trottiscliffe
TRAINS	nearest stations Borough Green and Snodland
TERRAIN	woodland and arable land
SEASONAL SUITABILITY	late spring to late autumn
SURFACE	stone-based farm tracks, some rough woodland tracks
CLIMBS/DESCENTS	2 short steep climbs/ 2 gentle descents
REFRESHMENTS	The Plough PH and The George PH, Trottiscliffe

1 Turn right out of Trottiscliffe village hall carpark. 0.8 kms (0.5 miles) after passing Church Lane on the left, and shortly after a left hand bend, take the next right onto a broad stone track. Continue for 0.8 kms (0.5 miles).

2 At a fork of tracks follow the concrete track around to the left. Continue straight ahead past Coldrum Long Barrow, leaving the concrete track as it swings round to the right and continuing on a clay track.

The stones of Coldrum Long Barrow

3 Keep straight ahead as the track climbs. At a T-junction with a tarmac track, turn right and go straight ahead onto the North Downs Way.

4 Continue in the same direction for 3 kms (2 miles). For a straightforward there-and-back ride, turn round here. Otherwise turn right onto the road.

5 Continue downhill passing Paddlesworth Road on the left. Shortly after a left-hand bend, turn right onto a concrete track signposted 'Bridleway. Birling Place and Farm'.

6 Go through Birling Place and Coney Lodge Farm. At the third farm signposted 'Park Farm. Private' leave the concrete track and turn

sharply right onto the track signposted 'Bridleway'.

7 Climb for 0.8 kms (0.5 miles). At the T-junction with the North Downs Way turn left.

8 The track becomes tarmac. At a T-junction with a more major road turn right uphill then first left onto a track alongside a brick wall signposted 'Byway'.

9 Turn left downhill at the T-junction with a road then first left by a red brick house onto Wrotham Water Lane.

10 At the crossroads in Trottiscliffe go straight ahead into Church Lane, then left at the T-junction with School Lane to return to the start.

10 Ightham Mote

Toy's Hill, Ide Hill, and the High Chart are just some of the evocative names encountered along the North Downs. This circular route explores Ightham Common and Mereworth Woods, and passes the Iron Age fort at Oldbury Hill. The highlight of the ride is Ightham Mote, a perfect medieval moated manor house.

GRADE medium	
DISTANCE 22.5 kms (14 miles)	
TIME allow 3.5 hours	
MAP OS Landranger 188 Maidstone and the Weald of Kent	
GRID REF AT START 595566	
PARKING behind the village hall in Ightham	
TRAINS nearest stations Kemsing and Borough Green	
TERRAIN broadleaf woodland, fruit orchards, agricultural land	
SEASONAL SUITABILITY late spring to late autumn	
SURFACE sand based tracks, short rough sections	
CLIMBS/DESCENTS 1 steady, 2 steep climbs/ 1 steep descent	
REFRESHMENTS Chequers PH, George & Dragon PH, Ightham; Papermakers Arms, Rorty Crankle Inn (cream teas after 3pm), Plaxtol	

1 Starting in Ightham with your back to the Chequers PH, turn right, then right again onto Sevenoaks Road signposted 'Seal, Sevenoaks (A25)'. At the crossroads with the A25 go straight on past the Cob Tree PH. Continue for 0.8 kms (0.5 miles).

2 Where the road turns sharp left continue straight ahead onto 'No Through Road'. At the end of the tarmac take the left-hand bridleway just to the right of The Coach House alongside a low brick wall. Then follows a steep climb/push through a sand cutting. At

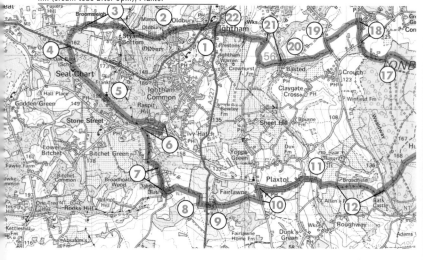

the top go straight over the crossroads of tracks.

3 This is a steep stony descent, possibly muddy. At the T-junction with the road turn right. At the T-junction by a 'Give Way' sign turn left uphill.

4 At the crossroads with the A25 go straight ahead signposted 'Stone Street, Bitchet Green'. After 0.8 kms (0.5 miles), after the clearing on the left and before the start of the descent, take the second of the two bridleways diagonally left.

5 The main track is muddy at times but there are usually parallel tracks offering firmer ground. Bear right at the road and then left onto the bridleway immediately after the church and the school. Continue for 1.6 kms (1 mile).

6 At the T-junction with a road, with a white house ahead, turn right,

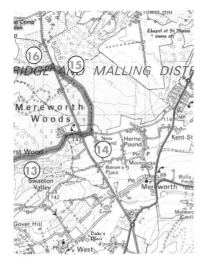

then right again at the T-junction with Stone Street. After 0.8 kms (0.5 miles), at a 'Stone Street' sign, turn left onto the bridleway.

7 A steep descent follows, at times stony. Turn right at the T-junction with the road by Mote Hill Cottage. Go past Ightham Mote then, opposite the red-brick farm, turn sharp left back on yourself, through the metal gates signposted 'National Trust. Ightham Mote. Bridleway'.

8 Go past the manor house. Continue on the track for 0.8 kms (0.5 miles). At the field gate turn right along the edge of the field. Turn left at the major track at the edge of the field.

9 At the crossroads with the A227 go straight ahead through the bridlegate signposted 'Fairlawne Estate'. At the T-junction with a pond ahead turn left, then first right sharply back on yourself through a field gate following a blue arrow. Go across open parkland past a tall yellow marker. Go through a bridlegate and into a second field.

10 Pass along an avenue of trees. At the T-junction with the road turn left, then first right by the Rorty Crankle Inn.

11 Go past Long Mill Lane and the telephone box and take the next right into Brook Lane, signposted 'Old Soar Manor'. At the next T-junction turn left signposted 'Old Soar Manor'.

12 On a sharp left-hand bend bear right (straight ahead) onto a track called Allens Lane for a long steady climb over 0.8 kms (0.75 miles). The track broadens. At the road go straight ahead onto a bridleway.

13 Go straight on, on a broad, improved surface through coppiced woodland.

14 At the crossroads with the B2016, by the Beech Restaurant, go straight ahead onto Beech Road. After 365 m (400 yds), opposite New Pound Lane and by a low metal barrier, turn left onto a track which can be rough at times.

15 Continue in the same direction for 0.8 kms (0.5 miles). At the T-junction turn left alongside a metal fence. The track narrows. At a crossroads by a house and some power lines turn left onto a broad drive. At the road turn right then take the first tarmac lane left by a tall metal railing signposted 'Bridleway'.

16 Go past some kennels. Continue onto a single track which soon runs parallel with a good track. Ignore a bridleway to the left which crosses the better, parallel track. The path soon improves, becoming a broad, stone-based track.

17 As the track swings left, passing a timber works on the right, take the next right sharply back on yourself before the 'Hurst Wood'

sign. Continue around the perimeter of the wood mill and onto a tarmac track.

18 At the T-junction with Long Mill Lane turn right. After the start of the houses in Platt, and immediately before a '30 mph' sign, turn left onto a track signposted 'Bridleway'.

19 Follow the bridleway along the field edge. The track turns to

The medieval manor house of Ightham Mote

tarmac. At the road go straight ahead through a narrow gap in hedge and turn left onto the track.

20 Follow the track around the field edge, turning sharp right at the bottom. The track climbs and descends through woodland for 1.2 kms (0.75 miles), with a short rough section near the end.

21 At the crossroads by the factory go straight ahead past the brick and stone Spring Cottage onto the bridleway. At the road turn right then after 0.8 kms (0.5 miles) turn first left signposted 'Ightham 3/4'.

22 At the T-junction at the end of Mill Lane turn right, then left to return to the start.

The North Hampshire Downs

Fine views are the main features of these two linkable rides which explore the Hampshire Downs. The Test Way and a liberal sprinkling of unclassified roads (UCRs) and roads used as public paths (RUPPs) ensure that you meet as few vehicles as possible.

11 Hurstbourne Tarrant

The first of the two rides passes through green lanes north of Hurstbourne Tarrant. They are particularly fine in spring adorned with May blossom and cow parsley. Autumn is beautiful too as the trees take on their golden colours.

GRADE	medium
DISTANCE	21 kms (12 miles)
TIME	allow 2.5 hours
MAP	OS Landranger 174 Newbury and Wantage and 185 Winchester and Basingstoke
GRID REF AT START	383532
PARKING	some parking along B3048. Ask permission to park in pub carpark
TRAINS	nearest station Whitchurch
TERRAIN	mostly arable land; chalk downland, woodland
SEASONAL SUITABILITY	all year, muddy in deepest winter
SURFACE	almost all good stone-based tracks
CLIMBS/DESCENTS	1 long steep climb/1 long steep and several shorter descents
REFRESHMENTS	George & Dragon PH, Hurstbourne Tarrant; Crown Inn, Upton

1 Start at the George & Dragon PH in Hurstbourne Tarrant. Take the road signposted 'Ibthorpe'. Go through Ibthorpe, then 365 m (400 yds) after the last houses turn left onto a track between hedgerows for a steady climb over 2.5 kms (1.5 miles), past a mast and onto tarmac.

2 At the T-junction with the road turn left. Continue for 0.8 kms (0.5 miles)

3 Turn right at the crossroads towards 'Tangley, Chute' (your right of way). After another 0.8 kms (0.5 miles), on a sharp left-hand bend bear right (straight ahead) then bear left (also straight ahead) onto the track for 0.8 kms (0.5 miles).

4 At the T-junction with a narrow tarmac lane turn right, then right again, onto a track for a good descent.

5 At the crossroads, with farm buildings on the right, go straight ahead.

6 Turn left downhill at the T-junction with a road. At the T-junction in Upton, by a triangle of grass and a

The Test Way north of Ibthorpe

telephone box, turn right, then left signposted 'Linkenholt'. After 0.8 kms (0.5 miles) take the first track left uphill after Upton Manor. Ignore a left fork near the beginning of the hill.

7 At the T-junction with a road bear right past some wooden barns. Bear left (straight ahead) at the next T-junction signposted 'Vernham Dean' then after 50 m (55 yds) bear right onto a track.

8 Go straight ahead at the crossroads of tracks. Then go past Box Farm onto a tarmac track. At the T-junction by a row of flint cottages and a triangle of grass, turn right. On a sharp left-hand bend, near power lines, turn right onto a track.

9 At the crossroads of tracks go straight ahead. The track turns to tarmac and goes through Littledown, passing the Methodist chapel on the right. Turn left at the T-junction with a thatched house ahead called 'The Boot', then turn right signposted 'Linkenholt'.

10 At the T-junction just past Linkenholt church on the left, turn right signposted 'Upton, Andover' ✚.

11 On gentle descent, 0.8 kms (0.5 miles) after last farm buildings, turn left onto the track signposted 'Test Way'.

12 90 m (100 yds) after passing beneath power lines, turn left at the crossroads of tracks, signposted 'Test Way'. Continue for 2.5 kms (1.5 miles).

13 Shortly after a sausage-shaped black barn, at the T-junction of tracks, turn right. Pass to the left of the farm. At the T-junction with a tarmac track by tall yew hedge, turn left. Then at the T-junction at the end of Horseshoe Lane turn left to return to the start.

✚ **Link 3** To link with Inkpen Hill, ride no 12, turn left signposted 'Faccombe, Combe'. After 1.2 kms (0.75 miles), near the bottom of the hill and 50 m (55 yds) before the road junction turn sharp left onto a track signposted 'Bridleway'. Join the Inkpen Hill ride between directions 3 and 4.

12 Inkpen Hill

In addition to views over the valley of the River Kennet you may well come across paragliders soaring above you with brightly coloured parachutes on the second of the North Hampshire Downs rides.

GRADE medium	
DISTANCE 14.5 kms (9 miles)	
TIME allow 2 hours	
MAP OS Landranger 174 Newbury and Wantage	
GRID REF AT START 370620	
PARKING Inkpen Hill carpark on the minor lane leading SE from Hungerford. Follow signs for Combe and Linkenholt, towards Inkpen and Walbury Hill	
TRAINS nearest station Kintbury	
TERRAIN chalk downland, woodland, arable land and pasture	
SEASONAL SUITABILITY late spring to late autumn, muddly after rain	
SURFACE quiet lanes, good stone-based tracks, some rough sections	
CLIMBS/DESCENTS 1 long steady climb/1 fast descent	
REFRESHMENTS nothing on route; pubs at Faccombe, Upton and Vernham Dean just off the route	

1 From the carpark turn right on the track climbing away from Combe Gibbet. After almost 1.6 kms (1 mile) at the end of the broad track bear right along the road for 1.6 kms (1 mile).

2 After passing a mast, as the road swings left, bear right onto a track signposted 'Byway' for a fine 2.5 km (1.5 mile) descent.

3 At the junction with the road go straight ahead signposted 'Linkenholt, Andover' ✚ then after 50 m (55 yds) bear right signposted 'Bridleway'. Follow the valley floor track passing a small red-brick barn on the right and ignoring left and right turns. Where the valley appears to fork go straight ahead signposted 'Test Way'.

4 At the end of an open access field bear slightly left signposted 'Bridleway' onto the easiest track ahead. The gradient steepens and the track turns to tarmac.

5 At the T-junction, with a large red-brick house ahead, turn right past the telephone box. Continue for 0.8km (0.5 miles).

6 On a sharp left-hand bend, by triangle of grass, turn right onto a 'No Through Road'. Bear left as the tarmac ends. At the T-junction with a ridge track turn right. The track improves towards the top.

7 Go over Inkpen Hill back to the start.

✚ **Link 1** To link with Hurstbourne Tarrant, ride no 11, turn left at the road junction signposted 'Netherton, Hurstbourne Tarrant'. Continue for 0.8 kms (0.5 miles), turn right by triangle of grass with metal chain onto a tarmac track, then fork left alongside a flint and tile wall.

✚ **Link 2** Climb for 1.2 kms (0.75 miles). At a T-junction of tracks turn right uphill away from the 'Footpath' signposted left. At the T-junction, with power lines ahead, turn left signposted 'Right of Way'. 90 m (100 yds) after passing beneath power lines turn left at the crossroads of tracks signposted 'Test Way'. Join ride no 11 between directions 11 and 12.

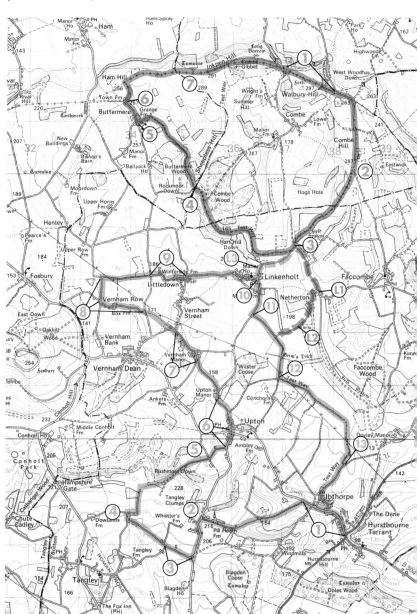

13 King's Wood

Good quality tracks through one of the best of the Forestry Commission's Kent holdings are the attraction of this route. It descends into the delightful village of Chilham where good pubs, teashops and a castle can be found. It is a good idea to carry a compass as timber operations can alter routes as new tracks are created and old ones obliterated.

All tracks, T-junctions and crossroads mentioned in the directions below are broad, stone-based forestry tracks not narrow earth tracks.

GRADE	easy/medium
DISTANCE	16 kms (10 miles)
TIME	allow 2.5 hours
MAP	OS Landranger 189 Ashford and Romney Marsh
GRID REF AT START	024500
PARKING	King's Wood carpark, on minor road signposted 'Wye' which forks left off A251 just south of Challock
TRAINS	nearest station Wye
TERRAIN	undulating forestry tracks
SEASONAL SUITABILITY	all year
SURFACE	stone-based forestry track, small rough patch
CLIMBS/DESCENTS	1 major descent and 1 major climb
REFRESHMENTS	teashops and pubs in Chilham

1 Turn right out of King's Wood carpark and go 365 m (400 yds) along the road towards Challock. Just before the A25 turn right by gates and take the track for 0.8 kms (0.5 miles).

2 Take the second of the two tracks to the right (NE direction) for a gentle descent.

3 At a five-way junction of tracks, with an 'Oathill Riding School' sign to the left and a 'Dogs on lead' sign to the right, go straight ahead.

4 Go past a green corrugated iron shed. At the first major crossroads at the bottom of the hill go straight ahead.

5 At the second major crossroads go straight ahead downhill.

6 At the third major crossroads turn left to continue descending.

7 Go down then up. At the T-junction with red marker ahead turn left onto the North Downs Way (turn right for a shorter route and rejoin between directions 11 and 12.)

8 At the T-junction by the metal gate and wooden bridlegate turn right downhill.

9 The track swings sharp left at the bottom of the hill. At the road go straight ahead downhill into Chilham. To return to King's Wood start in the square: with the castle entrance ahead,

turn left, then bear right at the T-junction signposted 'No Through Road'. Continue for 1.6 kms (1 mile).

10 As the road bears left to Hurst Farm go straight ahead onto a track signposted 'No cars, motorbikes except access. North Downs Way'. The track swings right uphill. At the top, turn left through the wooden bridlegate which is adjacent to the metal field gate and a 'No cars' sign. Follow the signs for North Downs Way.

11 Follow the North Downs Way past a red dot marker on a wooden post.

12 At the next North Downs Way marker, where the trail turns sharp left – there is also a gate into a field 45 m (50 yds) ahead – leave the North Downs Way and turn right onto an earth track. It may be muddy in parts but only lasts 275 m (300 yds). At the T-junction with a major track turn left. Continue for 1.2 kms (0.75 miles).

13 At the T-junction bear left, then at the T-junction with a road, by a Forestry Commission 'King's Wood' signpost, turn right to return to the start.

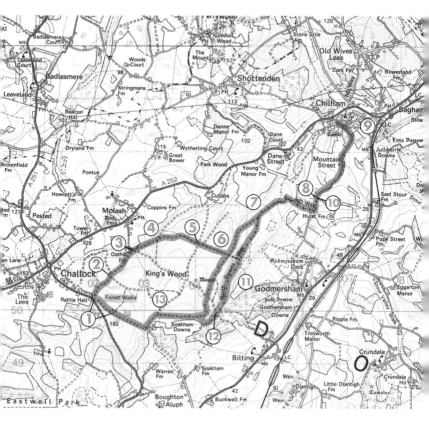

14 Forest Way

A fine circular route using a dismantled railway and two stretches of bridleway either side of the lofty summit of Crowborough. Views over Ashdown Forest, home of Winnie the Pooh, the River Medway and, in late spring, gardens full of rhododendrons, azaleas and laburnum provide a varied but peaceful ride.

GRADE medium

DISTANCE 30.5 kms (19 miles)

TIME allow 3 hours

MAP OS Landranger 187 Dorking, Reigate and Crawley and 188 Maidstone and the Weald of Kent

GRID REF AT START 531373

PARKING opposite the Post Office in Groombridge; turn off the B2110 at Victoria PH signposted 'Eridge, St Thomas Church. Post Office is 135 m (150 yds) on right

TRAINS nearest station Eridge

TERRAIN woodland, orchards, cutting and embankments

SEASONAL SUITABILITY late spring to late autumn

SURFACE tarmac lanes, broad tracks, dismantled railway

CLIMBS/DESCENTS 1 long, 1 steep and 1 short climb/1 steep and 1 fast descent

REFRESHMENTS Victoria PH, Crown PH in Groombridge; Hatch Inn, Coleman's Hatch

1 With your back to Groombridge Post Office turn left on Corseley Road away from the shops.

2 Cross the stream then cross the railway bridge. After 0.8 kms (0.5 miles) turn first left by a triangle of grass onto Forge Road signposted 'Eridge Station'. Continue for 2.5 kms (1.5 miles).

3 Easily missed! Take the road right signposted 'Holdens. Bullfinch Farm'. Go straight on past Mott's Farm and ignore a right turn to Bullfinches.

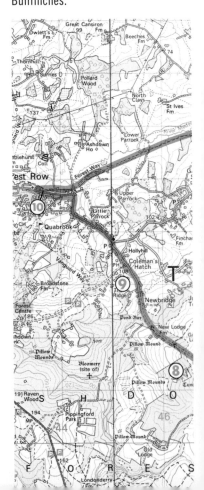

© Crown Copyright

4 Keep on the main track past some orchards as it becomes tarmac at Gillridge Farm. At the next road turn left then first right onto Ghyll Road. At the end of Ghyll Road turn right then left onto Old Lane. Continue for 1.6 kms (1 mile).

5 Easily missed! Go past the flowering shrubs in gardens of large houses for 1.6 kms (1 mile). Turn right at the crossroads onto Warren Road – if you come to a T-junction at the end of Melfort Road you have gone too far. Continue for 1.6 kms (1 mile).

6 At a triangle of grass by Home Farm and Clock House, bear left downhill onto a track for a fast descent followed by a long, steady climb.

7 At the T-junction with the B2188 go straight across by a barrier onto a wide grassy track. At the T-junction with a major track turn left then go diagonally right across a concrete and grass track with unusual star-shaped holes. Follow this track towards the road.

8 At the junction with the B2026 go straight ahead onto the lane

opposite signposted 'Newbridge, Colemans Hatch, Forest Row'.

9 A fast and furious descent on tarmac, followed by a steady climb, passing the Hatch Inn. At the T-junction just past the pub turn right, then turn left signposted 'Forest Row, East Grinstead'. At the T-junction by a large church turn left downhill. Continue for 2 kms (1 25 miles).

10 Shortly after a petrol station, opposite Post Horn Lane and a telephone box, turn right onto a gravel track signposted 'Bridleway'. At the T-junction with the Forest Way turn right and continue for 5 kms (3 miles) *or* turn left for East Grinstead.

11 At the T-junction immediately after a large yellow stone bridge turn left, then right.

12 Cross the minor road near Balls Green, continue for (2.5 kms (1.5 miles), then soon after crossing a bridge with a water tap at a fork of tracks bear right downhill on shallow steps. At the T-junction with the road turn left.

13 After 1.6 kms (1 mile), where the B2128 joins from the right, turn right onto a track between houses. At the T-junction with tarmac by a pine tree turn left and return to the start.

The trail at Groombridge

15 Ditchling Beacon to Lewes

This stretch of the South Downs Way is one of the best. You may feel you have grown a pair of wings on this exhilarating ride which provides views out to the Channel and north across the Sussex Weald. There are two possible starting points, Clayton windmills and Lewes.

GRADE medium/ medium to hard

DISTANCE 14.5 kms (9 miles)/29 kms (18 miles)

TIME allow 1.5 hours/3 hours

MAP OS Landranger 198 Brighton and the Downs

GRID REF AT START 303134

PARKING carpark near Jack and Jill Windmills, off A273

TRAINS nearest stations Lewes, Falmer

TERRAIN open chalk downland

SEASONAL SUITABILITY South Downs Way all year; other sections late spring to late autumn

SURFACE stone-based, short rough sections

CLIMBS/DESCENTS 2 moderate climbs, 1 steep climb/ 3 descents

REFRESHMENTS pubs and teashops in Lewes; pub in Falmer

1 From the carpark the track goes uphill past the windmills towards Ditchling Beacon 3 kms (2 miles) away.

2 At the road at Ditchling Beacon follow the South Downs Way (SDW) straight ahead, then take main ridge route towards the highpoint of Blackcap.

3 Soon after passing the trig point (see Navigation) at Blackcap fork right. Continue for 2 kms (1.25 miles).

4 At another fork of tracks, close to a farm, bear right onto the broad track passing close to the farm (may be muddy in winter and after wet weather). Follow this track downhill towards a tall round chimney on the outskirts of Lewes.

5 At the junction with A275 turn right, (to visit Lewes go straight ahead. ★) then at the crossroads by traffic lights go straight ahead signposted 'Kingston 2, Rodmell 4, Piddinghoe 6'.

6 At the T-junction, by the Swan Inn, turn right signposted 'Kingston, Rodmell, Piddinghoe' then right again onto Juggs Road. Cross the bridge over the A27. Here tarmac turns to track and the section through the field may be muddy in winter and after rain.

7 The track turns back to tarmac near the farm. At a crossroads with a road go straight ahead signposted 'Kingston Ridge'. The hills loom ahead. Take the right hand fork.

8 Now comes a steep climb on a sunken chalk track. At the top, as the main track peters out take the right fork to the gate at the far end of the field. Continue for 0.8 kms (0.5 miles).

9 Take the first track right, signposted 'South Downs Way,' leaving the broad track that leads towards the mast.

10 Easily missed! At a junction of three metal gates, leave the SDW by turning left, continuing downhill on the left hand side of the fence. The track swings left.

11 At the T-junction with the B2123 turn right downhill, along a busy section for 1.6 kms (1 mile).

12 At the mini-roundabout go straight ahead over the bridge over the A27. At next mini-roundabout go straight ahead signposted 'Falmer North, University of Sussex', then turn first right onto Mill Street signposted 'Falmer North. Playing Fields'. At the T-junction with Ridge Road turn left signposted 'Playing Field, Pavilion' ◆ After 1.2 kms (0.75 miles) at a fork bear left, signposted Shambledean Bottom.

13 At the fork of tracks just past St Mary's Farm bear right. Continue for 2.5 kms (1.5 miles).

14 At the T-junction at the top of the hill, shortly after Streathill Farm, turn left onto the SDW which takes you back to the start 5 kms (3 miles) away.

★ Alternative start from Lewes: follow the signs for the A275 past the war memorial in the centre of town. At the traffic lights, soon after the Black Horse PH and the Pewter Pot PH, turn left signposted 'Kingston, Rodmell, Piddinghoe' and onto the main route at direction no 6.

◆ SC If you started in Lewes and want a short cut back bear right at fork after 1.2 kms (0.75 miles) signposted 'Waterpit Hill ¾ mile'. Follow the main track to the top of the ridge ahead near to Blackcap, turn right and rejoin the route at direction no. 3.

The South Downs near Ditchling

16 Arundel to Bignor Hill

The Roman road of Stane Street once ran from London to Chichester. A section of the ancient route is used on this ride of diverse landscapes, including a river section along the River, one of only three rivers to cut through the South Downs. An ideal refreshment stop is the pretty village of Slindon.

GRADE	Medium to hard
DISTANCE	26 kms (16 miles)
TIME	allow 3 hours
MAP	OS Landranger 197 Chichester and The Downs
GRID REF AT START	018071
PARKING	Arundel: use signposted carparks
TRAINS	nearest stations Arundel and Amberley
TERRAIN	river valley, chalk downs, mainly wooded
SEASONAL SUITABILITY	late spring to late autumn, muddy in winter and after prolonged rain
SURFACE	stone-based tracks, rough narrow woodland tracks, roots on river section
CLIMBS/DESCENTS	1 long, 1 short climb/1 long, 1 short descent
REFRESHMENTS	lots of pubs and teashops in Arundel and just off route in Amberley; Black Rabbit PH, Offham; The George & Dragon PH, Houghton; Newburgh Arms PH, stores in Slindon

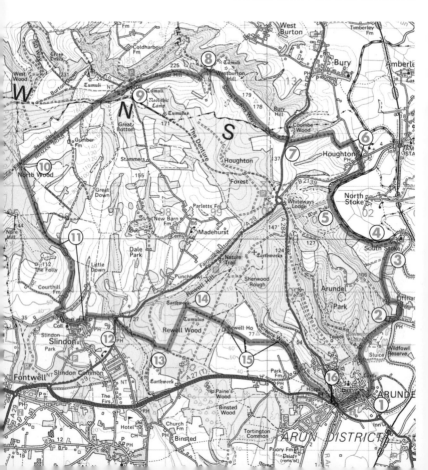

1 With your back to the Norfolk Arms PH in Arundel turn left. At the mini roundabout turn left into Mill Road. Go past the castle and lake.

2 At the Black Rabbit PH bear left onto 'No Through Road'. At the next T-junction turn left signposted 'Stoke only'.

3 Easily missed! Just before the red-brick barns of South Stoke Farm turn left onto a track signposted 'Bridleway'. After 50 m (55 yds) turn left by the barn signposted 'Bridleway'.

4 Follow the bridleway uphill around the edge of the field – this section may be rough, you will probably have to push. Go through the gate and down through woodland to the River Adur.

5 The section along the river is slow because of roots crossing the path. Chalk cliffs are to the left. The track turns to tarmac.

6 At the T-junction with the B2139 turn right, then immediately left signposted 'Bury'. After 0.8 kms (0.5 miles) take the first track left sign-posted 'South Downs Way'. Climb steeply for 1.6 kms (1 mile).

7 At the T-junction with the busy A29 turn right then left and follow the South Downs Way (SDW) for 2.5 kms (1.5 miles).

8 At the bottom of a hill just past a barn on the right, the route jiggles left then right, and climbs steeply up onto Bignor Hill.

9 At the carpark/wooden signpost showing Latin names, go through the wooden barrier in the direction of 'Noviomagus'. Follow along the upper side of the woodland (not towards the mast). After 180 m (200 yds) at a fork of tracks bear right. Continue through a bridlegate which is next to a field gate. This is the old Roman road of Stane Street.

10 Follow Stane Street into the wood, at the six-way junction of tracks turn left 90 degrees – taking the wooden bench in the clearing as a bearing, take the track slightly to the right of the lengthwise direction of the bench. Continue for 2 kms (1.25 miles).

11 At the T-junction where the track turns to tarmac bear right. At the T-junction with a road turn left into Slindon, going past the church. Take the next left after Slindon Pottery signposted '6ft 6ins width limit'.

Riding the South Downs Way

12 Just before the T-junction with the A29, turn right signposted 'Chichester' then go straight across the A29 onto the bridleway opposite. Continue for 1.2 kms (0.75 miles).

13 At a big junction of tracks turn sharply left uphill towards a wooden barrier. Ignore right turns and follow the 'Bridleway' signs.

14 At a three-way bridleway sign go straight ahead.

15 Emerge from woodland and bear left onto a wide stone track (not the sharp left turn alongside the woodland). As the main track swings right downhill go straight ahead along the field edge. Continue in same direction, pass through three gates and into woodland. Bear right signposted 'Bridleway' for a long descent.

16 At tarmac turn right, then at the roundabout take the second exit onto Maltravers Street signposted 'Town Centre' to return to the start.

17 Chanctonbury Ring

A tough but rewarding ride starting in Findon and taking you past one of the most magical spots along the whole South Downs Way – the panoramic viewpoint on the wooded hilltop of Chanctonbury Ring.

GRADE difficult	
DISTANCE 32 kms (20 miles)	
TIME allow 4 hours	
MAP OS Landranger 197 Chichester and The Downs and 198 Brighton and The Downs	
GRID REF AT START 122088	
PARKING in Findon, near the shops or in road signposted 'Chanctonbury, unsuitable for motors'	
TRAINS nearest stations Arundel and Amberley	
TERRAIN downland, rough sections, open field	
SEASONAL SUITABILITY South Downs Way and east of A24 all year, first 3 miles muddy late autumn to late spring and after prolonged rain	
SURFACE mostly good stone-based tracks, muddy field in winter	
CLIMBS/DESCENTS 4 tough climbs/4 good descents	
REFRESHMENTS Village House PH, Gun Inn, Black Horse Inn, teashop and food store in Findon; George & Dragon, Burpham; Frankland Arms, Washington	

1 In the centre of Findon, with your back to the Gun Inn, turn right towards the main road. Just before the T-junction with the A24 bear left opposite the Black Horse PH onto a No Through Road. Then turn right through a gap in the fence to cross the A24 (take care) onto a concrete track opposite, signposted 'Rogers Farm, bridleway'. After 180 m (200 yds) leave the concrete track and turn right onto a gravel track signposted 'Bridleway'.

2 Climb through woodland. At a T-junction turn right signposted 'Bridleway'.

3 At the crossroads with the A280★ go straight across signposted 'Tolmare Farm'. After 30 m (33 yds) bear left downhill and immediately left again signposted 'Bridleway'.

4 Descend then climb on a broad track that will be muddy in winter. Go straight across an open field which will be very sticky in winter.

5 Go along the next field edge. At the T-junction with a better track turn left, then right signposted 'Bridleway. Myrtle Grove Farm. No Through Road'. Go through the farm. At the T-junction, with flint and brick farm office ahead, turn left then right onto track signposted 'Bridleway'. This section may be muddy in winter.

Chanctonbury Ring impressive despite the Great Gale of 1987

6 The track surface improves alongside a tall brick and flint wall. At the T-junction with tarmac turn right uphill.

7 Follow this road for 5 kms (3 miles), through Lee Farm and continue as the surface changes from concrete/tarmac to track.

8 At the T-junction turn right, then fork right going the opposite way to a 'Public Footpath' signposted left.

9 At the end of the first field turn left signposted 'Bridleway'. At the bottom of the hill ◆ turn left signposted 'Bridleway' for a fine descent.

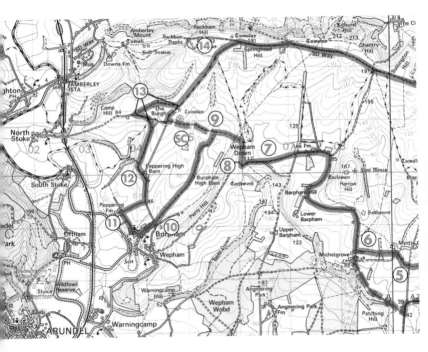

10 Go straight across at the junction with the road into Burpham. Go past the George & Dragon PH. With a 'No Through Road' and The Forge straight ahead, turn right.

11 Turn right at the T-junction by Peppering Farm, then at the T-junction by large triangle of grass turn left signposted 'No Through Road. Bridleway'.

12 At a fork by Peppering High Barn bear left onto a gravel track.

13 Bear left at the next fork . At the T-junction, with flint walls and barns on the left, turn sharply right. At the next T-junction turn left for a steady 2.5-km (1.5-mile) climb.

14 Bear right onto the South Downs Way (SDW) and follow SDW signs for 5.5 kms (3.5 miles) descending to the A24.

15 Cross the very busy A24 with care. Continue uphill on the SDW ignoring a right turn to Frieslands Farm near the start of the hill.

16 At the T-junction at the top of the steepest climb of the ride, the SDW continues left.

17 Go past the earthworks and trees of Chanctonbury Ring. Descend for 3 kms (2 miles). With the road in sight 300 m (330 yds) away, at a crossroads of tracks next to a flint memorial to Walter Langmead, turn right for a fast descent.

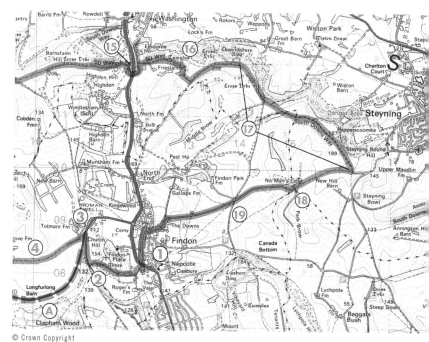

© Crown Copyright

18 At the junction of tracks at the bottom of the hill, bear slightly right uphill onto the steeper of the two tracks ahead.

19 Go straight ahead at the crossroads of tracks by a wooden-fenced field, keeping the fence to your left. Follow this track downhill into Findon, turning right at the bottom to return to the Gun Inn.

★ **A** Autumn to spring/wet weather alternative. To avoid an open field turn left at the A280 for 3 kms (2 miles) then take the second road right to rejoin at direction no. 6.

◆ **SC** For a short cut, at bottom of the hill continue straight ahead. At the T-junction turn right and follow this track to the SDW. Turn right onto the SDW to rejoin the route between directions no. 13 and 14.

The chalk trail near Wepham Down

18 Glorious Goodwood

The South Downs offer the best, challenging off-road cycling in the southeast of England. This ride explores the woodland to the north and east of Goodwood race course. You loosen up with a flat road section before you start to climb.

GRADE Medium to hard	
DISTANCE 22.5 kms (14 miles)	
TIME allow 2.5 hours	
MAP OS Landranger 197 Chichester and The Downs	
GRID REF AT START 936120	
PARKING 2 carparks at Selhurst Park Forestry Commission on the minor road off the A285 between Petworth and Chichester, signposted Singleton 6, Midhurst 12	
TRAINS nearest station Amberley	
TERRAIN woodland, downland, arable land planted with grain	
SEASONAL SUITABILITY late spring to late autumn	
SURFACE broad stone-based tracks, 1 field	
CLIMBS/DESCENTS 2 main climbs/3 descents	
REFRESHMENTS Fox PH, Charlton	

1 Start at the Selhurst Park Forestry Commission carpark. Turn right out of the carpark and follow the road for 3 kms (2 miles).

2 At the crossroads (your right of way) go straight ahead. Shortly after passing Counters Gate/ Goodwood Country Park carpark on the left, bear right onto a track signposted 'No cars beyond this point' (NB do not take the footpath which is to the right of this). Go past glorious Goodwood racecourse to your left on a long thrilling descent.

The picturesque village of Charlton

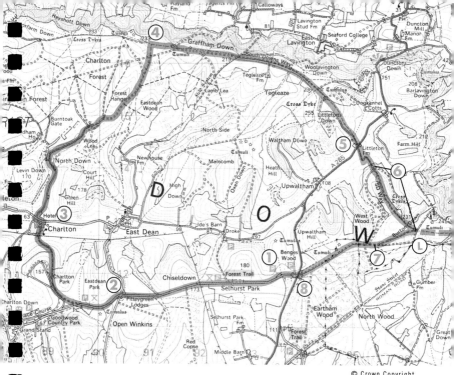

3 Turn left at the T-junction in Charlton by the Fox PH, then first right signposted 'Downs bridleway. Unsuitable for motors'. A 165 m (550 ft) climb over 4 kms (2.5 miles) follows on excellent quality track. Go straight ahead at several crossroads of tracks.

4 At the top of the climb, at the T-junction, turn right onto the South Downs Way (SDW) for a lovely undulating section on good quality track for 5 kms (3 miles). Keep following the SDW. The gradient steepens as you drop through a field to the road.

5 At the junction with the road turn right, then left continuing on the SDW.

6 After 0.8 kms (0.5 miles) fork right and continue climbing. At the T-junction at the top of the hill, with radio masts to the left and the SDW ahead, turn sharp right back on yourself ✚.

7 Bear right at the T-junction with a more major track. Follow this downhill for 1.6 kms (1 mile).

8 At the T-junction with the A285 go straight ahead onto a road signposted 'Singleton 6, Midhurst 12' to return to the start.

✚ **Link** For a link to Arundel to Bignor Hill, ride no. 16, go straight ahead on the SDW to the carpark and a wooden signpost with Latin names and join the other ride at direction no. 9.

19 Harting Downs

This ride carries a 'difficult' grading because of the number of climbs and the surface of the track. It is challenging but rewarding and provides some invigorating views over the South Downs. North of the tumuli (direction no. 8) requires some tricky navigation through a plethora of woodland tracks. A compass would be useful.

GRADE difficult	
DISTANCE 26 kms (16 miles)	
TIME allow 3.5 hours	
MAP OS Landranger 197 Chichester and The Downs	
GRID REF AT START 791181	
PARKING Harting Downs carpark	
TRAINS nearest station Rowland's Castle	
TERRAIN open downland, farmland and woodland	
SEASONAL SUITABLITY late spring to mid autumn	
SURFACE mixture of stone-based and earth tracks with some rough sections	
CLIMBS/DESCENTS 2 long, hard climbs/several short climbs/two long descents	
REFRESHMENTS Hare & Hounds PH, Stoughton; White Horse PH, Chilgrove	

1 Harting Downs carpark is at the top of the steep hill on the B2141 between Petersfield and Chichester. Turn left out of the carpark onto the B2141 towards Chilgrove. Easily missed: 365 m (400 yds) after a small parking area on the left (National Trust Harting Downs Nature Reserve) on a fast tarmac descent, turn right by a white wooden post onto a broad stone and chalk track alongside beech trees.

2 After 90 m (100 yds), fork left signposted 'Bridleway', stay close to the right-hand edge of the next two fields, the track is rough. Then the track crosses to the other side of the hedgerow and improves in quality.

3 At the junction with a lane, go straight ahead and climb past houses to the top of Telegraph Hill following the bridleway signs. The bridleway crosses a footpath. Bear slightly left keeping to the bridleway. Here the track improves and passes beneath power lines.

4 Turn left at the T-junction with the road. After almost 1.6 kms (1 mile) and shortly after double green metal gates on the right, take the next track left signposted 'Bridleway'. This is the access road to Keeper's Cottage.

5 At a T-junction of tracks turn right signposted 'Bridleway' for a long single-track descent through woodland. At the crossroads with a road go straight ahead uphill onto a track.

6 Turn right at the T-junction in Stoughton (or turn left for Hare & Hounds PH) then after 180 m (200 yds) turn left between a house called

© Crown Copyright

'Jeremys' and Tythe Barn House onto a concrete track signposted 'Bridleway'. Climb through woodland on a broad stony track for 1.6 kms (1 mile).

7 50 m (55 yds) after a low breeze block construction on the right, in a clearing, take the next track left signposted 'Bridleway'.

8 Emerging from the woodland at the tumuli, bear to the right and continue on a track parallel with the one you have been following which continues climbing. Keep going over several crossroads of tracks, eventually bearing right by a wooden gate into yew trees. The bumpy track improves with a better stone base.

NB. From the tumuli to Chilgrove there are many woodland tracks and it is easy to get lost. Using your compass, from the tumuli, Chilgrove lies to a point between north and north-north-east.

9 Go through a bridlegate next t a wide gate. At the T-junction with another broad track turn right downhill for a fast descent into Chilgrove.

10 By the White Horse PH, at the T-junction with a busy road, turn right then after 365 m (400 yds) turn first left. At the crossroads turn left signposted '6ft 6ins width limit'.

11 At Stapleash Farm turn sharply right signposted 'West Dean' then after 180 m (200 yds) take the first track left through a metal gate signposted 'Bridleway' into woodland where the surface improves. Climb steadily for 2.5 kms (1.5 miles).

12 At the top of the climb, at the T-junction with the South 'ns Way (SLW), turn left for a gentle :cent over 3 kms (2 miles).

13 Easily missed! At the crossroads of tracks turn right signposted 'South Downs Way', descend, then a short climb.

14 At the T-junction turn left, then turn first right signposted 'South Downs Way'. After 1.2 kms (0.75 miles) turn left steeply uphill signposted 'South Downs Way' for 0.8 kms (0.5 miles).

15 Turn right for a long, fast descent. At a crossroads of tracks by a tall wooden post in a large grassy clearing, turn left uphill signposted 'Buriton, South Downs Way' and follow this back to the start.

Written by: Nick Cotton
Editor: Melanie Sensicle
Location photography: Nick Cotton
Designed by: Martin Lovelock
Production manager: Kevin Perrett
Managing editor: Miranda Spicer
Project manager: Kevin Hudson

Nick Cotton has asserted his right to be identified as the author of this work.

First published 1995

© Haynes Publishing 1995

Published by:
Haynes Publishing
Sparkford, Nr Yeovil, Somerset BA22 7JJ

British Library Cataloguing-in-Publication Data:

A catalogue record for this book is available from the British Library.

ISBN 1 85960 113 8

Printed in Great Britain